FAITHS FOR THE FEW

By the same author:

FAITHS FOR
THE FEW
A Study of Minority Religions

WILLIAM J. WHALEN

THE BRUCE PUBLISHING COMPANY
MILWAUKEE

NIHIL OBSTAT:
>> JOHN F. MURPHY, S.T.D.
>> Censor librorum

IMPRIMATUR:
>> ✝ WILLIAM E. COUSINS
>> Archbishop of Milwaukee
>> April 26, 1963

Library of Congress Catalog Card Number: 63–19634

© 1963 WILLIAM J. WHALEN

MADE IN THE UNITED STATES OF AMERICA

PREFACE

Popular writers often divide the American people into three neat religious categories: Protestants, Catholics, and Jews. Pollsters confirm this categorization because most Gentile non-Catholics identify themselves as "Protestants" when asked their religious preference.

Nevertheless a tri-faith United States does not correspond with reality. Secular Humanism certainly constitutes a commitment, a faith, a way of life for many millions of Americans. Its values and assumptions and moral attitudes do not coincide with those of any of the three major theistic religions. Eastern Orthodoxy, likewise, claims the spiritual allegiance of 2,500,000 Americans and the two main Latter-day Saints bodies report nearly 2,000,000 members.

Beyond these obvious exceptions to the familiar tri-faith description of American religious life are many other minority religions. Some of these such as Baha'i and the Nation of Islam (Black Muslims) are related to another world faith: Islam. Some, such as Theosophy, Rosicrucianism, and the I Am cult, are generally classified as occult religions. Others, popularly identified as Protestant denominations, such as Christian Science and Jehovah's Witnesses, actually bear only a superficial resemblance to historic Protestantism and, in fact, negate the basic principles of the Reformation.

These minority faiths range in size from the moribund Swedenborgian Church of the New Jerusalem with fewer than 7,000 adherents in this country to the prosperous, mushrooming Church of Jesus Christ of Latter-day Saints (Mormons). Many of these bodies originated and developed in nineteenth-century America even though they now count a majority of their followers outside the United States. For example, Jehovah's Witnesses, a cult founded in Pittsburgh and now headquartered in Brooklyn, reports three members outside the United States to every American Witness. The Baha'is have attracted only 12,000 American converts but number millions of members in Iran and India. The same preponderance of non-American followers is reported by the Spiritualists, Seventh-day Adventists, Moral Re-Armament enthusiasts, and Old Catholics.

We have also included a discussion of the Philippine Independent Church (Aglipayan) since that church was founded in American-occupied territory and has spent most of its short history under the American flag. American citizens were influential in giving this schism theological and political direction. Today the Aglipayans maintain intercommunion and close ties with the Protestant Episcopal Church from which it received Anglican orders in 1946. Its supreme bishop claims 2,500,000 followers including some Filipinos in Hawaii.

Some of the minority religions we will discuss date back to the early eighteenth century while others, such as the I Am and Black Muslim movements, originated as recently as the 1930's. Of course, many sects and cults have come and gone over the years. They lacked the power of survival and have become historical curiosities. The celibate Shakers are an example of a near extinct cult while the mail-order cult of Psychiana died with the death of founder Frank Robinson.

While a few cults like Swedenborgianism and I Am are stagnant, some far outdistance the older established denominations in growth. Jehovah's Witnesses, for instance, has been termed the fastest growing religion in the world; in the 20 years between 1942 and 1962 membership increased 700 per cent and now approaches 1,000,000. The Utah Mormons carry on an extensive missionary campaign with the aid of 12,000 volunteer missionaries who are usually young men just past 19. Last year the Mormons baptized 105,000 converts, double the harvest of the previous year. This together with an unusually high birth rate, stable family life, and low death rate has pushed the Utah-based church into the forefront of American cults.

Even excluding the four million Freemasons and the Aglipayans, the adherents of the various minority religions described in the following chapters would easily exceed 5,000,000 in the United States and Canada. If a study in depth were undertaken to discover the genuine commitment of a sampling of American adults, we might find that Secular Humanism alone would claim 20 or 25 million "believers." Regardless of "church-preference" statistics, four out of ten Americans lack even a nominal affiliation with any church or synagogue.

Not all minority religions are included in this book. Other chapters might have considered Vedanta, the Hutterites, Father Divine's Peace Mission, the Christadelphians, Anglo-Israelism. We have tried to concentrate on those groups which are fairly well known among Catholics and Protestants. Relatively speaking we have sometimes devoted more attention to groups about which little has been published such as the Rosicrucians, Polish National Catholics, Old Catholics, Aglipayans, and Liberal Catholics and less to such well-researched groups as Christian Science.

Most of the cultists described in these chapters engage in active proselytism; they are branded sheep stealers since they usually work among people already within some Christian tradition. They use the printed word, door-to-door preaching, reading rooms, radio and TV, mass rallies to bring their message to the people. For example, the Witnesses now print four million copies of their semimonthly Watchtower and three million of Awake! This is several times the circulation of the largest Roman Catholic or Protestant periodicals. The average Witness also spends 11 hours a month in doorstep preaching. Each local Christian Science branch is expected to maintain a reading room where the writings of Mary Baker Eddy and the Christian Science publishing society are available.

The cultists are daily visiting Catholic and Protestant homes and presenting their own often bizarre doctrines. Their efforts are bearing fruit. Thousands who once attended Sunday Mass with their fellow Catholics now stand on the street corner selling copies of the Watchtower or find their spiritual nourishment in a Mormon sacrament meeting or a Baha'i study circle.

The Christian, lay or clerical, who knows nothing about the cults can offer little help to other Christians among his family, neighborhood, or acquaintanceship who may be lured by the promises and attractions of the cults. To provide further study about any particular group we have included a selected bibliography. Only books in English normally available in public libraries of medium and large cities and in universities have been listed.

Some of the chapters in this volume originally appeared as magazine articles. All such chapters have been revised and enlarged. I would like to thank the editors of *The Priest, Sign, Mary Immaculate,* and *The Lamp* for permission to use this material.

A number of individuals have been kind enough to review specific chapters. In particular I would like to thank Mr. Peter F. Anson, Sr. Mary Dorita, B.V.M., Mr. Richard L. Pierce, Rev. Richard Ginder, Rev. John A. Hardon, S.J., and Rev. Leo A. Piguet. Prof. Eric L. Clitheroe examined the complete manuscript and offered many valuable suggestions. Mrs. Ruth Shaffer did much of the typing. I would also like to thank my wife for her patience, critical readings, typing assistance, and helpful comments.

W. J. W.

February 1, 1963
Lafayette, Indiana

CONTENTS

ix

FAITHS FOR THE FEW

CHAPTER 1

DOUKHOBORISM

Russian Spirit Wrestlers
Plague Canadian Authorities

———— • ————

American husbands who "get mad" at their wives are likely to put on their hats and coats and leave the house. The Sons of Freedom sect of Doukhobors who "get mad" at the government are likely to take off all their clothes and burn down their houses.

For more than 40 years the Sons of Freedom have battled the Canadian government. Trouble started when the government seized some Freedomite land as payment for fines incurred when the members of the sect refused to send their children to school.

In 1962 the Sons of Freedom outdid themselves in arson and bomb attacks. They climaxed their series of destructions by blowing up a 366-foot power transmission tower on the east bank of Kootenay Lake, throwing 1000 people out of work because of the power loss. A few weeks later the Royal Canadian Mounted Police rounded up all the Freedomite leaders, charging some with terrorism and 70 others with masterminding the raids and with "conspiring to intimidate Parliament."

While the Sons of Freedom languished in jail their wives and daughters set out on a scorched earth policy at their main village of Krestova. They reduced the 110 houses to fewer than a dozen tar-paper shacks.

Another protest device of the Sons of Freedom is nudity. They maintain that nudity simply expresses their religious view that man is a naked child, but they also know that such demonstrations embarrass the authorities and bring attention to their cause. Freedomites have paraded in the nude, danced in the nude while setting fire to their buildings, and ridden 35 miles in a railroad box car to jail — in the nude. When 50 Sons of Freedom were convicted of public nudity in 1950 they quietly listened to the reading of the sentence and then proceeded to remove their clothes in the packed courtroom.

We should understand that the Sons of Freedom is only one sect of the Russian mystical movement known as Doukhoborism. Only 2000 or so of the estimated 18,000 Doukhobors in British Columbia and other Canadian provinces belong to this fanatical wing.

Most of the minority religions described in these chapters developed within Roman Catholicism or Protestantism. Doukhoborism arose as a protest against the Orthodox Church of Russia, as did such other sects as the Raskolniki, Khlysti, Skopsti, Molokani, Stundists, and Pashkovites which are generally unknown to Western Christians.

Doukhoborism began in Kharkov and the villages of Dnieper in eighteenth-century Russia when groups of peasants rejected the authority of the established Orthodox church and appealed instead to the authority of the "inner light." In this and some other respects they resembled the Quakers and they would later be befriended by English and American Quakers.

The Doukhobors believed in God but denied the Christian doctrine of the Trinity. Jesus was simply a man who lived many years ago and who possessed wisdom and virtue to an unusual degree. Neither the Bible nor the Church was a reliable guide to spiritual perfection; only the inner voice could lead man to this goal.

Their name — Doukhobors — means Spirit Wrestlers. The Orthodox priests and civil authorities insisted that the dissidents were wrestling against the spirit of God, whereas the believers maintained they were wrestling for the spirit. They turned their backs on the priests, icons, rituals, and sacraments of Russian Orthodoxy. They likewise spurned the schools, the taking of oaths, and military service. They would follow the dictates of their consciences and the direct guidance they received from God. Their plain board altars held only a pitcher of water, a dish of salt, and a loaf of bread. They greeted each other with "Slava bohu" (The Lord be praised).

A basic contradiction in Doukhoborism has been their firm assertion of the freedom and independence of the individual coupled with their eager acceptance of spiritual dictatorship. Often the dictator was far from spiritual himself. One of their early leaders was Saveli Kapustin who was acknowledged as such in 1790. He had declared: "As truly as the heaven is above me and the earth beneath my feet, I am the true Lord Jesus Christ."

From the beginning of their revolt the Doukhobors were hounded by the czar's officials who wanted them to serve the usual terms as conscripts in the Russian army. They refused to bear arms and threatened, if conscripted and pressed into battle, to shoot their rifles into the air above the enemy's heads.

Czar Alexander I, a more liberal ruler, allowed the Doukhobors to settle in the Milky Waters area bordering the Black Sea. Here they prospered, established model villages, and paid their taxes. Only occasional brushes with the authorities over suspected proselytizing among the Orthodox marred their efforts to build a utopia. In 1817 the Doukhobors reported the death of Kapustin but many believe that he simply went into hiding and continued to direct the sect for several years from his refuge.

Kapustin's son, Vasili Kalmikoff, succeeded to the leadership of the sect but became a drunkard and died in 1832. His son, Illarion Kalmikoff, was also dissolute and let the apostles and elders manage the affairs of the community. He was a bachelor but the elders desired a male heir to the spiritual throne so they supplied him with six virgins. Two sons were born in this experiment.

While Illarion loafed, cavorted with his mistresses, and drank vodka the elders instituted a reign of terror. Debauchery, secret murders, feuds rent the Doukhobor settlements. The government finally declared, "In the name of your religion and by the command of your pretended teachers, you put men to death, conceal crimes committed by your brothers, and hide information from the government." They were banished to the Wet Mountains of the Caucasus.

Illarion's son, Peter Kalmikoff, assumed the role of "Christ" after his father's death and following family tradition spent most of his hours drinking, hunting, and sleeping. He married a 16-year-old girl, Lukeria Vasilivna Hubanova, and passed the spiritual leadership to her before he died. "I give you to Lukeria. The spirit of Christ will pass from me to her," he told his faithful Doukhobors. At 28 he was dead. By this time the number of Doukhobors had risen to about 10,000.

The son of a well-to-do Doukhobor family, Peter Vasilivich Verigin, had caught the eye of Lukeria many years before when he was just a lad. In the meantime he had married another girl by the name of Dunia. Lukeria was annoyed at his marriage and induced him to divorce his young bride and live with her. A month after Peter left his wife she gave birth to a boy, Peter Petrovich Verigin, who would one day assume the leadership of the Doukhobors in Canada — with disastrous results.

Conditions in the Doukhobor villages did not improve. Superstition, magic, dream interpretations were prevalent. The government began to draft Doukhobors for three-year army terms, considerably shorter than the usual 25-year period for other conscripts. When Lukeria died, Peter Vasilivich tried to take over control but not all Doukhobors recognized his authority. The villages divided into the so-called "Mad Doukhobors" and the "Bad Doukhobors."

In 1886 Peter was arrested for agitating against the state and was exiled to Archangel province, about 1500 miles from the main Doukhobor settlements. He continued to direct Doukhobor affairs by letter although his power was unknown outside the Doukhobor communities. The Doukhobors had learned to use evasion and deceit in talking to outsiders. They answered all questions about their organization by repeating: "We have no leader, none among us is greater than another. We are all brothers and sisters in Christ."

In exile Peter absorbed the writings of Leo Tolstoy and incorporated these into Doukhoborism. He became a vegetarian and by letter directed the Doukhobors to follow suit. He directed them to redistribute their wealth and establish a communal system. He advised against the use of tobacco and liquor and finally forbade sexual intercourse. Hundreds left the movement when they heard of this latest regulation. The government moved Peter further from the Doukhobor faithful by sending him to Siberia.

Tolstoy encouraged the Doukhobors and protested their persecution and Peter's exile to the authorities. His naïve assessment of the real nature of the sect indicates he knew little about the true role of Peter Vasilivich Verigin:

> The Doukhobors are a most remarkable people. They work with their hands, exploiting no one, producing more than they consume. They reject authority of both church and state, acknowledge no human authority, yet live together peacefully in their community with no guidance other than their own reason and conscience. Among these dignified, confident, yet illiterate peasants, is the germination of that seed sown by Christ himself 1800 years ago.

One letter from Peter told the believers: "Christ wants you to burn your guns!" They collected all their rifles, pistols, and swords, poured oil and fat on the mountain of weapons and set them afire on June 29, 1895. This angered the Cossacks who descended with whips and clubs on the hymn-singing Doukhobors gathered around the bonfire. Now the government broke up the Doukhobor settlements, sending some to the swamps of Batum while others wandered about the Russian countryside. Many died of whippings, disease, and malnutrition.

Verigin and his Doukhobor counselors decided to seek refuge in some other country. Assisted by English and American Quakers they negotiated an arrangement with Canada which was looking for immigrants. The first boatload of Doukhobors arrived in 1898; the Canadian government has had difficulties with the Russian mystics ever since.

The Russian government refused to allow Peter Vasilivich Verigin to accompany the Doukhobors to their new homeland. He continued to send letters but his advice was typically vague and ambiguous. He never rescinded his ban on marriage and sexual intercourse but the Doukhobors resumed their old habits in Canada.

When Verigin finally managed to leave his Siberian exile and reached Canada in 1902 he saw clear evidence of disintegration of the Doukhobor movement. Some Doukhobors in Saskatchewan had left the communal living plan and obtained land of their own. They were known as Independents. Another group, forerunners of the Sons of Freedom, objected to the Canadianization of their children or any compromise with the state. Verigin's own Christian Community of Universal Brotherhood faced serious problems brought about by mismanagement, excesses, indecision.

The arrival of the exiled leader boosted the morale of all the Doukhobors. He managed to obtain loans for land and equipment. In 1909 and 1910 he led most of the Doukhobors from Saskatchewan to British Columbia where they are concentrated to this day. Here they planted thousands of fruit trees, irrigated the land, built sawmills and brick factories. They started a jam factory at Brilliant and soon B. C. Jam was well known in Canadian pantries. (Eventually the jam factory, pride of the Doukhobor community, would burn to the ground, the object of an arsonist's torch.)

Peter sent for his divorced wife Dunia and his 24-year-old son, Peter Petrovich Verigin. The young man — foulmouthed, arrogant, cruel, and lewd — spent his days in Canada discrediting his father's claims to religious leadership. The Doukhobors accepted his abuse and vices with the thought that God works in mysterious ways. After a few months his father sent him back to Russia.

On October 28, 1924, Peter Verigin boarded a Canadian Pacific train with one of his many mistresses. Both were blown up in the middle of the night when a dynamite bomb went off under Verigin's seat. Seven other passengers were killed in the explosion. The crime was never solved. More than 10,000 Doukhobors attended his funeral; his grave remains a shrine although it too has been the object of bombing attacks.

Peter Petrovich Verigin returned to Canada from the U.S.S.R. and his arrival split the Doukhobors into further schisms. His gambling, drunkenness, and stupidity combined with the economic effects of the Great Depression and the expensive arson and bombings dragged the settlements into bankruptcy.

More than 600 Sons of Freedom were tried for nudity, arson, and perjury in 1932 and were confined on Piers Island, two miles off the coast of Sidney, Vancouver Island. The government had to put the prisoners on the island since the jails were already full of Freedomites. They also imprisoned Peter Verigin.

Verigin died in 1939. Despite his conduct he had managed to hold the allegiance of some Doukhobors. World War II further disorganized the Doukhobor community. High wages and good prices for lumber and farm products drew the Doukhobors from the communal system and today no Doukhobors are living under the original, Tolstoyan plan. Most Doukhobor children now attend public schools and a few have even gone on to college and entered the professions. Another Verigin, John, directs the heirs of the Christian Community of Universal Brotherhood which is now called the Union of Spiritual Communities of Christ. His authority is less secure than that of the two Peters because of the possible existence of an uncle in the U.S.S.R. The uncle has not been heard from in years and has become a mythical character.

The Sons of Freedom display the most intense reaction to Canadian life. They still resist the education of their children in public schools and continue their protest by nudity, arson, and bombings. Several years ago the Sons of Freedom threatened to go back to Russia to which the Canadian government replied in effect: "Wonderful. Can we help you pack?" But the Sons backed down and the problem for the Canadians remained. Recently many of the Freedomites have accepted the leadership of one Stefan Sorokin who came from Uruguay and has since returned to self-exile in South America. He sends regular proclamations and directions to the Freedomites. Should he attempt to return to British Columbia the police have warrants for his arrest on a number of charges. Sorokin's followers call themselves the Christian Community and Brotherhood of Reformed Doukhobors.

In recent years nine other countries besides Russia have turned down proposals to accept the cantankerous Sons of Freedom: Cuba, Turkey, Peru, Chile, Colombia, Brazil, Uruguay, Venezuela, and Argentina. Commented Robert Bonner, attorney general of British

Columbia: "We don't want to unload our troubles on another country, but I don't know what to do with these people."

Plagued by dissolute leaders, schisms, and the fanaticism of the Sons of Freedom the Doukhobors have been unable to maintain their communal way of life in Canada. The materialistic attractions of Canadian life and the democratic attitude of the Canadian government do not provide the same soil for growth as did the oppressive czarist regime of eighteenth- and nineteenth-century Russia. Doukhoborism seems to lack the ingredients to guarantee survival and the sect is unlikely to see the twenty-first century.

CHAPTER 2

SWEDENBORGIANISM

Swedish Seer Swedenborg
Sought Solace in Spirit Sphere

———— • ————

Movie and theater goers who watched the Irish nurse Anne Sullivan, break through to the dark world of the little girl in *The Miracle Worker* might be surprised to learn that when that little girl grew up she joined one of the oldest and oddest of the Christian cults: Swedenborgianism. Helen Keller, now 82 and a famous author, is a Swedenborgian.

Although far older than such cults as Mormonism and Christian Science and tiny in comparison to their memberships, Swedenborgianism has exerted an influence on these and other religious movements which would be hard to overestimate. Spiritualism, Mormonism, New Thought have all felt the impact of Swedenborgian theology.

Swedenborgians follow the curious doctrine of an amazing scientist-turned-theologian, Emanuel Swedenborg (1688–1772). The two U. S. branches of this faith enroll fewer than 7000 adherents and the cult is otherwise confined to England, Australia, and a few foreign missions.

Swedenborg, born in Stockholm, was raised a Lutheran. In fact his father was chaplain to the king and later Lutheran bishop of Skara. Emanuel was a brilliant student who received a doctorate from Upsala at 21, toured Europe, and threw himself into many fields of science. Before turning to religion at the age of 55 he had authored 60 books and papers in various scientific areas.

This latter-day da Vinci was a professional philosopher, physicist, geologist, metallurgist, mathematician, botanist, musician, zoologist, astronomer, mining engineer, chemist, physiologist, bookbinder, clockmaker, lens grinder, editor, and mineralogist. Charles XII appointed him assayer of mines in 1716.

Henry James called Swedenborg the "sanest and most far-reaching intellect this age has known." Thomas Carlyle said of him: "A man of great and indisputable cultivation, strong, mathematical intellect, and the most pious, seraphic turn of mind; a man beautiful, lovable, and tragical to see . . . . One of the loftiest minds in the realm of mind." Balzac, Coleridge, Emerson, and the Howells all discussed the ideas of Swedenborg. The Swedish seer also influenced Kant and Goethe whose *Faust* represents the Swedenborgian world view.

After this remarkably fruitful career in the sciences and government services, Swedenborg issued a claim that he was able to converse with inhabitants of the spirit world. In 29 books on religion, including his *True Christian Religion*, he described in minute detail the flora and fauna of heaven, hell, and the intermediate spirit world. His writings were all in Latin and the complete set fills two or three library shelves.

Swedenborg reported lengthy conversations with Luther, Melanchthon, and Calvin. He persuaded Luther that he had been wrong about his ideas of faith without works. One of Swedenborg's "discoveries" was that marriage continues after death with some possible reshuffling of mates, while the unmarried like himself may find their soul mates in the next world.

The Swedish theologian declared that the Old Testament, four Gospels, and Book of Revelation were authoritative but that St. Paul and Luther were in error. He devised an allegorical interpretation of the Bible. In his system cities in the Bible always typify systems of belief, stones stand for truth, houses are intelligence, snakes are carnality, etc.

He denied the Trinity. Jesus Christ was God Himself and the Trinity represented three aspects of Christ. He claimed that Jesus appeared to him in 1745 and introduced him to the spiritual meaning of Scripture.

At death men go to the realm where they will feel most at home. It may be heaven, hell, or the spirit world which is a sort of purgatory. The other world is much like this one and men go about doing what they like to do, living in houses, etc. He was also sure that other planets were inhabited by races of men far superior to those on earth.

The Last Judgment was not to come. It had come in 1757 and had been witnessed by Swedenborg himself. He especially hated the Protestant doctrine of justification by faith alone which, he said, was the great red dragon of revelation. However, despite his quarrels with orthodox Lutheranism he never left the church; he quit attending services because the spirits constantly interrupted the sermons to correct the preachers' mistakes.

He went to England in 1771 and remained there until his death a year later. For many years he had moved from Stockholm, to Amsterdam, to London, and back. In 1908 his body was returned to Sweden where it is buried in the cathedral in Upsala.

His writings antedated modern spiritualism by almost a century but certainly gave direction to the spiritualism spawned by the Fox sisters in 1848. Prof. Emeritus Charles Braden of Northwestern points out that Swedenborg's books were well known at this time and prepared many people to accept spiritualism.

His ideas on eternal marriage found permanent roots in the marriage doctrines of the Mormons. The latter marry not for time but for time and eternity. Swedenborg was revered as a "divinely illuminated seer and revelator" by his followers; Joseph Smith took the title "prophet, seer, and revelator" of his new church.

Warren Felt Evans, a Swedenborgian clergyman healed by Phineas P. Quimby, wrote two books on mental healing before Mrs. Eddy was able to get her own *Science and Health* to press. She certainly knew Evans' theories which were colored in part by his Swedenborgianism.

Swedenborg himself never founded a church. About a dozen years after his death a group of Englishmen including two Anglican preachers, Thomas Hartley and John Clawes, organized the Church of the New Jerusalem. The movement won converts in the Lancaster area. It spread to America in 1792 and societies were established around Baltimore. A church was set up in 1817. In 1890 a large number of Swedenborgians in Pennsylvania left the original group and established a second branch. In general the New Church has been confined to the Atlantic seaboard.

The original group, known as the General Convention of the New Jerusalem in the United States of America, claims only 4070 members in 56 churches. It operates a tiny theological seminary at Cambridge, Massachusetts. Well endowed by some wealthy members it can offer seminary training for an annual tuition of only $25 and provides free room and board to ministerial candidates, single or married. The student body rarely numbers more than four. There are 32 ordained Swedenborgian ministers.

This older branch also controls the Swedenborg Foundation of New York City which publishes and distributes Swedenborg's writings. A modest advertising campaign to acquaint Americans with the teachings of the cult is also financed by the Foundation.

The smaller General Church of the New Jerusalem maintains headquarters at Bryn Athyn, Pennsylvania. It supports 12 churches, a seminary, and academies for boys and girls. Its current membership is given at 1805. The General Church claims to adhere more closely to Swedenborg's theology and accords him more divine honor than the older branch. It has a mission in South Africa.

The English Swedenborgians number about 7000. The two American groups are barely holding their own. In fact the General Convention reported more members in 1911 — 8500 — than it does today. Despite efforts at proselytizing, the cult seems unable to interest many in Swedenborg's dreams and allegories.

Miss Keller, who called Swedenborg "one of the noblest champions true Christianity has ever known," was converted to Swedenborgianism early in her life. She declared that he had found "the word of God . . . freed from the blots and stains of barbarous creeds." Her friends, the Macys, thought Swedenborg was a bit crazy, and, when Helen referred to the seer Anne Sullivan Macy rebuked her saying, "You know perfectly well you're talking moonshine."

A number of other Americans have been Swedenborgians, including the father of Henry and William James who was a Swedenborgian clergyman, the financial expert Barron, poet Vachel Lindsay, landscape painter George Inness, and popular newspaper poet Edgar Guest.

The liturgy of the New Church is based on the Anglican Book of Common Prayer. The church celebrates the Lord's Supper four times a year. It baptizes infants as well as adults and confirms adult believers. The best known Swedenborgian church is probably the Wayfarers' Chapel at Portuguese Bend, California. Designed by the son of Frank Lloyd Wright, the chapel is built of glass supported by redwood girders. It is the picturesque scene of many weddings, some from the movie colony.

The Church of the New Jerusalem seems doomed to extinction. It has difficulty holding its own adherents much less winning converts to Swedenborg's bizarre notions. Americans are likely to dismiss the Swedish seer as a brilliant scientist who "flipped." Still Swedenborgianism has had its influence on American religious life and directly on several flourishing cults. It cannot be ignored in any consideration of contemporary religious sects.

CHAPTER 3

FREEMASONRY

Masons Adhere to Doctrines and Morals of Naturalism

———— • ————

Most Masons joined the lodge for business and social reasons. Nevertheless the lodge illustrates all the characteristics of a religious sect and it is chiefly on this basis that it is condemned by the Catholic Church and other Christian bodies.

If only one Mason out of 20 takes the religious and cultic aspects of the lodge seriously, we are dealing with a body of 200,000 American men. Worldwide Freemasonry enrolls 5,500,000 members of whom four million live in the United States. At least 200,000 find in their lodge all the dogmas, ritual, fellowship, and moral code which others find in churches and synagogues.

All the Masonic legends about King Solomon's Temple to the contrary notwithstanding, the Masonic lodge as we know it can be traced to a meeting of four vestigial masonic lodges in a London tavern in 1717. During the Middle Ages Christian masons formed trade unions known as lodges and employed certain passwords and grips in lieu of a union card.

After the Protestant Reformation cathedral building suffered a decline and these lodges of working masons began to initiate honorary or nonworking masons to bolster sagging lodge rosters. Eventually these honorary masons took over the apparatus of the lodges and formed what we now know as Speculative Masonry.

These modern lodges spread to the continent and to areas colonized by the English. Today the majority of the world's Masons are English-speaking. What has become a mass organization in the

United States remains an elite corps in Europe and Latin America. The typical European Mason is frankly anticlerical, probably agnostic, urbane, sophisticated, proper, circumspect. He values his Masonic membership as a rare privilege and advances in the lodge only through a system of strict surveillance, education, and invitation by his Masonic superiors. He wears no Masonic pin, seldom advertises his meeting places, and as a continental rather than an English Mason makes no attempt to combine any brand of Christianity with Masonic naturalism.

Transplanted to American shores shortly after its English birth, Freemasonry served as a convenient vehicle for the colonial revolutionaries. In the secrecy of the lodge room they were able to discuss their growing dissatisfaction with English rule. Many of the famous men of the American Revolution wore the Masonic apron: George Washington, Paul Revere, Benjamin Franklin, Alexander Hamilton, and Patrick Henry, to name a few. Most of these men would be considered Deists rather than orthodox Christians.

What served well during a revolution drew the suspicion of Americans struggling to establish democratic processes. The abduction and presumed murder of Captain Morgan, who threatened to expose Masonic secrets, aroused the nation. Thousands of Masons burned their aprons in disgust, Masonic publications suspended operation, lodges closed their doors during the 1830's. An Anti-Masonic political party presented slates in many eastern states and saw a few of its candidates win office.

After the Civil War secret societies entered a golden age in the United States. The most outlandish rituals were concocted by the inventive organizers of such societies as the Knights of Pythias, KKK, Sons of Temperance, and the like. Almost every American male who was free, white, and 21 belonged to one or more such lodges. Masonry shed the stigma of an earlier era, and in the decades that followed it became the undisputed champion of the secret-society system. Most of the lodges which were founded in the 1880's and 1890's have faded to insignificance, but Masonry today enrolls more brothers than ever before in its history.

Masonry managed to survive the demise of dozens of American

secret societies and fraternal orders. Some offered insurance benefits which they combined with rituals usually so banal that we
find it hard today to understand that they once moved the
hearts of grown men. But so did *East Lynne* and *Uncle Tom's
Cabin*. The Odd Fellows and the Knights of Pythias, which once
competed for the loyalty of American joiners, no longer attract
young blood and seem to be withering away.

Now the wheel has begun to turn again and even though Masonry
counts its members by the millions it no longer attracts the diploma
elite, the organization man, the scholar, or the scientist. Younger
men see little prestige in climbing the Masonic degree ladder as
their fathers and grandfathers did. Not since 1948 has the American voter been able to cast a ballot for a Masonic presidential
candidate. Eisenhower, Stevenson, Kennedy, and Nixon are all non-
Masons.

Vance Packard, in his best selling *The Status Seekers*, comments
that the Masonic lodge has lost its appeal to the upper classes
and now draws its chief support from the "limited-success" class
of tradesmen, civil servants, mechanics, and the like. The inheritors
of wealth, the scholars and scientists, the corporation executives,
even the politicians no longer see much prestige in membership
in a 4,000,000-member Masonic lodge.

Certainly Masonry can still point to hundreds of brethren
prominent in national life, but most of these are middle-aged or
elderly gentlemen. Perceptive Masons in candid moments regret
the lack of interest in the lodge by younger men.

Masonic authorities such as Frank Land and Charles Van Cott
estimate the active Masonic membership at perhaps 10 per cent of
the total. Land, founder of the DeMolay order for boys, maintains
that 92 per cent of those who go through the three-degree initiation
never show up again for a regular lodge meeting.

All Masons belong to a local Blue lodge which confers the three
basic degrees of Entered Apprentice, Fellowcraft, and Master
Mason. A Mason may then decide to advance in the Masonic
hierarchy by either or both of the so-called higher rites: York or
Scottish. The former leads to the flamboyant Knights Templar who

wear plumed hats and military uniforms. The Knights Templar bar all Jews. The Scottish rite consists of 29 additional degrees culminating in the 32nd degree and the purely honorary 33rd. Only Knights Templar and 32nd degree Masons may join the Shrine, the playground of Freemasonry.

Master Masons who wish to become 32nd-degree members of the Scottish rite pay a fee of about $150, take a few days off from work, and spend them watching the enactment of the degrees at some Scottish rite cathedral. As many as 400 men go through these degrees at one time, which means they sit around a stage and watch playlets performed by special degree teams.

Regular Masonic lodges in this country forbid the initiation of women, Negroes, young men under 18, cripples, atheists, and the senile. Preaching brotherhood and fraternity, the 16,000 white lodges refuse to initiate any Negroes or to recognize the Masonic legitimacy of the Negro Prince Hall lodges. As a result Negroes have organized their own parallel lodges, York and Scottish rites, Shrine, Eastern Star, etc.

Masonry involves a network of 60 affiliated groups which depend on Masonic membership or relation to a Mason in good standing. These include the Eastern Star auxiliary for women, the Rainbow Girls and Job's Daughters for girls, DeMolay for boys, Acacia fraternity for college men, the National Sojourners for military officers, the Grotto and Tall Cedars of Lebanon for fun-loving Master Masons. Incidentally the Church's condemnation of lodge membership extends also to all these affiliated Masonic bodies.

Military officers above the rank of warrant officer may join the National Sojourners, Masonic organizations for active and retired officers, which enrolls 17,000 members. Masons in the military branches assisted in the reorganization of German and Japanese Masonry. Although careful records are kept of Masons in the Army, Navy, and Air Force, we have no evidence that anything resembling the infamous French affair des fiches exists in the United States. The exposure of this Grand Orient plot to advance only Masons and discredit non-Masons contributed to the demoralization of the French army before World War I.

Politicians still find some value in Masonic membership, although in certain areas of the country such membership is becoming more a liability than an asset. In 1957, 54 out of 96 senators were Masons including Sparkman, Smathers, Tallmadge, Dirksen, Capehart, Humphrey, Symington, Bricker, Kerr, Morse, Thurmond, Gore, Kefauver, Byrd, and Wiley. In the House of Representatives there were 212 Masons and 223 non-Masons. In the same year 31 out of 48 governors were lodge members.

Thirteen American presidents have been Masons including Washington and Harry S. Truman. Truman holds a primacy of honor among American Masons since he has served as Grand Master of Missouri and holds practically every Masonic degree and honor.

Prominent U. S. Masons have included William Jennings Bryan, Samuel Gompers, John J. Pershing, Irving Berlin, Fiorello La Guardia, Andrew Mellon, J. C. Penney, Henry Ford, Earl Warren, Paul Blanshard, Gen. Douglas MacArthur, Charles Lindbergh, and J. Edgar Hoover.

In the United States the lodge enrolls one out of every dozen adult males. This remarkable expansion is but one of many reasons why the American lodges have become an object of contempt to English and continental brethren. Its blatant racism, ridiculous Shrinerism, vulgar displays, mediocre leadership, and pitiful intellectual level combine to give foreign Masons the impression that the American lodges constitute a degenerate form of "pure and ancient Freemasonry."

Maintenance of Masonic membership, as we have seen, does not depend on regular attendance at lodge meetings. A man may go through the initiation ceremonies on several evenings and pay his dues by mail from that time on. To the outside world he is known as a Mason by his lapel button or ring, but his Masonic indoctrination has been limited to the memorization of his part in the rituals of the initiatory degrees. His continental counterpart would advance slowly and painfully from one degree to the next only after periods of intensive Masonic study and examination.

To be perfectly frank, the wonder is that anyone goes to the trouble of joining the average Masonic lodge today. The Craft's initiation system is so arranged that a lodge can seldom induct more than two or three Master Masons in a single evening. Hence, where 30 or 40 men join the local lodge during a year the weekly meetings must be devoted to the familiar degree work. The fun of putting friends and neighbors through the three degrees wears pretty thin after a few months and those who have served their time climbing the ladder to the Worshipful Master's chair may be so tired of the business that they show up again only for the annual Past Master's night or New Year's Eve dance.

Many people of good will fail to understand why the Catholic Church bars her sons from joining the Masonic lodge. They know that their Catholic neighbors hold membership in such organizations as the American Legion, AFL-CIO, and Lions. Why, then, has the Church singled out the Masonic lodge for condemnation?

These people deserve a reasonable answer to their question. To them the answer that the Church forbids such membership is no answer at all. They want to know why the Church does what she does. Catholics, too, should want to know the reasons behind this stand.

A variety of false and foolish reasons has been advanced. Some observers imagine that the Church objects to the lodge because of the confessional; they suppose that the Masonic oath would destroy the frank relationship between priest and penitent. Self-righteous Masons sometimes maintain that their lodge represents enlightment and democracy while the Church seeks to enslave men's minds and souls.

Others chalk up the antagonism between Church and lodge to some longtime political feud which no longer has any meaning for Americans or American Catholics. They sometimes concede that the Church may defend herself against the admittedly atheistic and anticlerical Grand Orients of southern Europe and Latin America. They point to the differences between these Masonic bodies and Anglo-Saxon Masonry but do not realize that the Church bases her objections to the Craft on grounds other than those of atheism or anticlericalism.

One group, with perhaps a touch of paranoia, sees Masonic

machinations behind every anticlerical manifestation in American life. They subscribe to the demon or conspiracy theory which neatly reduces the most complex issues to the simplicity of identifying the particular conspirators.

Another minority pooh-poohs any suggestion that Masonry, at least in this country, amounts to anything more than a mutual benefit society. They wonder what the fuss is all about, and decide that the Church's severe condemnations of the lodge must be based on a confusion between the harmless American bodies and the atheistic Grand Orients of Europe. To them everything seems to happen by pure coincidence.

Canon 2335 of the New Code of Canon Law, the law by which the Church of the Latin rite is governed, states: "Those who enroll in the Masonic sect, or in other associations of the same kind, which plot against the Church or legitimate civil powers, incur by that very fact an excommunication which is reserved in a simple manner to the Holy See."

This means that a "Catholic" Mason may not receive the sacraments, act as sponsor at a baptism or confirmation, or be buried from a Catholic church or in consecrated ground.

Basically, the Church's objections to Freemasonry are two. First, Freemasonry constitutes a system of religious naturalism and as such opposes the revealed Christian truths. Second, the lodge administers solemn oaths which are not within its power to administer. Let us examine both of these chief objections.

Masons regularly deny that their lodge is a religion in itself. In fact we find Protestant ministers wearing the Masonic apron and serving as living examples to other brethren that the lodge could not conflict with Christian beliefs. We know, however, that people have a capacity for compartmentalizing their lives and living with a number of inconsistencies. We know too, if we have studied comparative religion, that many sects and cults seek to mask their religious orientation in order to seduce the unsuspecting adherents of another faith. The Rosicrucians, the Jehovah's Witnesses, and the Unity School of Christianity, to name a few, also deny their religious basis.

It would be more profitable to examine Freemasonry and see what it might lack to qualify it as a distinct religious sect. The Masonic Lodge demands acceptance of two basic dogmas: the existence of a supreme being called a Grand Architect of the Universe and the immortality of the soul. This is more than Buddhists and Unitarians and Reform Jews must subscribe to. (The Grand Orients have removed these dogmatic tests of membership and have taken the Bible out of their lodges; they are branded as heretical by Anglo-Saxon Masons.)

We soon discover that the Masonic lodge embraces all the features of a religion: temples, altars, prayers, worship, symbols, vestments, feast days, a code of morality, the promise of a reward after death, a burial service, and others. In fact, the dogmatic demands and ritualistic aspects of Freemasonry can be seen to be more elaborate than that of a number of liberal Protestant denominations.

Some Masons admit the religious character of the lodge but insist that somehow it is a Christian institution. A moment's reflection would dispel this notion. Obviously, the Jews, freethinkers, and Moslems who hold Masonic membership could legitimately object to any Christianization of the lodge as "un-Masonic." As a matter of fact, the name of Jesus Christ is never spoken in the lodge except perhaps inadvertently by some Protestant minister or layman who is invited to offer a closing prayer. Such action has repeatedly been criticized as improper by the various state Grand Lodges. Christian Masons are invited to check their "sectarian" theological views at the door of the lodge.

True, most lodges in the United States place a Bible on their altars. Some naïve Masons imagine that this puts the stamp of Christianity on the lodge. Even a passing acquaintance with Masonic law and literature, however, would reveal that the lodge uses the Bible merely as a symbol of sacred writing. The ritual calls only for a Volume of Sacred Law (or VSL) which might be the Christian Bible, the Koran, the Book of Mormon, the Vedas, or any other collection of "scriptures." No one can prove that the lodge accords to the Holy Bible any special divine authority or inspiration which it does not also grant to these other scriptures. A news item

in the New Age magazine tells about a lodge in India upon whose
altar rest the VSL's of six different religions to accommodate the
theologically heterogeneous brethren.

To summarize, then, the Catholic may not join the Masonic
lodge any more than he may join the Lutheran or Baptist
church and remain in good standing. This prohibition in no way
depends on whether Lutheranism or the Baptist church engages
in anti-Catholic activities. In the case of the lodge we must say
that an individual simply cannot worship the naturalistic Grand
Architect of the Universe on lodge night and the triune God
of Christianity on Sunday morning. He cannot offer prayer in
the name of Jesus Christ on one day and suppress the name of
his Redeemer while praying with unbelievers the next.

Second, the Church must forbid her sons to take the solemn
Masonic oaths which climax the degree ceremonies. For Christians,
the taking of an oath has always been considered an act of religion.
Some Quakers and Mennonites even refuse to take an oath in court.
Catholics and most other Christians do not object to swearing an
oath for a serious reason when asked to do so by competent authority in the Church or State. They do not freely swear oaths in order
to join a fraternal society.

No Mason can swear these oaths without understanding perfectly
well that they are solemn oaths. He is blindfolded, kneeling before
the Masonic altar with his hands on the VSL. He repeats the oaths
after the Worshipful Master and consents to the most horrible
mutilation and death if he should ever reveal their contents or
betray their promises. For example, at the conclusion of the Master
Mason's oath the candidate swears:

> All this I most solemnly and sincerely promise and swear, with
> a firm and steadfast resolution to keep and perform the same
> without the least equivocation, mental reservation, or secret
> evasion whatsoever, binding myself under no less penalty than
> that of having my body severed in two, my bowels taken from
> thence and burned to ashes, and these scattered by the four winds
> of heaven, that no more remembrance might be had among men
> or Masons of so vile and wretched a man as I should be, should I

in the least knowingly violate or transgress this my Master Mason's oath. So help me God and keep me steadfast.

Clearly the Masons find themselves on the horns of a moral dilemma. If they take the oaths seriously, they are agreeing to mutilation and death which is immoral. If they do not take these oaths seriously, they must be judged guilty of taking the name of the Lord in vain.

No one with any curiosity about the subject denies that the secrets to which the Mason binds himself are known to all who take the trouble to discover them. You cannot keep ritual secrets in a mass organization of more than 4,100,000 men. Over a period of years, hundreds and thousands abandon the lodge, some join the the Catholic Church, and no longer feel obliged to observe an oath which the lodge had no right to impose. In order to conduct the degree initiations Masonic officers buy pocket-sized rituals printed in a simple code, no more difficult to decipher than the usual crossword puzzle. Bookstores sell these for $3.50 to any and all customers.

Millions of Protestant and Eastern Orthodox Christians share the attitude of the Catholic Church on lodge membership. In this country alone at least five million Protestants belong to denominations which forbid dual allegiance to Church and lodge. These bodies include the Missouri and Wisconsin Synod Lutherans, Christian Reformed, Salvation Army, Quakers, Mormons, Assemblies of God, Church of the Brethren, Church of the Nazarene, Free and Wesleyan Methodists, and others.

Of course, most American Protestants are either Baptists or Methodists and neither of these denominations forbid membership. What is more significant, however, is that no Christian denomination which has seriously examined the question of Freemasonry has come to any conclusion but to forbid or discourage membership.

Besides these two major reasons of religious naturalism and improper oaths, the Church objects to Masonry on other grounds. American lodges, it is true, do not share the bitter anticlericalism of the Latin and European lodges. The average American Mason may have no experience with anti-Catholicism in his local lodge. One of the so-called landmarks of the order forbids discussion of religion or politics within the lodge room. This rule, however, does not bind quasi-Masonic bodies such as the Scottish Rite. The Southern jurisdiction of the Scottish rite, enrolling 32nd-degree Masons in 33 southern and western states, has engaged in sustained anti-Catholic propaganda for many decades. Its vicious periodical, *New Age*, serves a steady diet of bigotry to 450,000 Masons.

This rule has also been violated in recent years by such groups as the Grand Lodge of California. The role of this Grand Lodge in the recent attempt to impose taxes on parochial and private schools has been exposed by such newspapers as the *Christian Science Monitor*. The voters of that state defeated the Masonic proposition by a two to one margin. Masonic support of Protestants and Other Americans United (POAU) and Christ's Mission for apostate priests has been well documented.

That thousands of fine gentlemen enroll in the lodges for business and professional and social reasons is undisputed. The Church has no quarrel with these men. If they attempt to combine the religion of the lodge with their Christian beliefs, we will not question their sincerity; we must, however, question their consistency. The great majority of Christians in the world today — Catholic, Protestant, and Orthodox — see no possible way to combine allegiance to Christ with allegiance to the lodge's Grand Architect.

CHAPTER 4

MORMONISM

Latter-day Saints,
Once Persecuted, Now Prosper

———— • ————

During the past decade the Mormon church almost doubled its membership and now claims approximately two million members in this country and foreign countries. The federal census in 1906 indicated a membership in the United States of only 256,647.

One out of three Latter-day Saints lives in Utah where members of the church form the majority of the state's 890,000 citizens. In a recent year this Church reported 105,000 adult conversions.

The Church of Jesus Christ of Latter-day Saints operates the largest church-related university in the nation: Brigham Young with 12,500 students on its sixty million dollar campus. An army of 12,000 dedicated young missionaries carries the bizarre doctrines of the Utah cult to every state and most foreign countries.

The once persecuted followers of visionary Joseph Smith, Jr., who were driven by enraged "Gentile" mobs from Missouri and Illinois, have prospered. They dominate Utah and wield increasing political and social power in Idaho, Arizona, and California. Converts and former westerners have formed wards (parishes) in most of the larger cities and university towns in the Middle West and East.

One of their Twelve Apostles, corresponding in authority to a cardinal, served as President Eisenhower's secretary of agriculture. Another Mormon has been chosen to be President Kennedy's secretary of the interior. Three Mormons serve in the United States Senate compared to nine practicing Catholics although Catholics outnumber Mormons 26 to 1 in the general population.

The Mormon church draws on the tithes of active members to build a commercial empire which embraces a department store, 360,000 acres of Florida cattle land, ranches and farms, mills, two insurance firms, an Hawaiian sugar plantation, radio station KSL, 72 downtown Salt Lake City buildings, sugar-beet refineries, a coal mine, newspapers, two hotels and a motel, and assorted factories. In addition, the Mormon church recently announced plans for a 30-story building in New York City to serve as eastern headquarters. To make it self-sustaining the building will also provide business offices and apartments for rental.

At one time the federal government stripped the church of all its property for defying the antipolygamy laws. Today no one but high LDS church officials knows the full extent of Mormon financial holdings. Secular businessmen in many industries make no moves without considering Mormon reaction; LDS officials sit on many corporate boards in which the church holds a substantial interest. Last year the church sold its controlling interest in Zion's First National Bank for a reported ten million dollars.

At present the United States government recognizes four major groupings of religions and issues appropriate "dog tags" for members in the armed forces: Catholic, Protestant, Eastern Orthodox, and Jewish. Continued Mormon growth and influence may well call for the addition of a fifth category of Latter-day Saints.

Mormonism cannot easily be pigeonholed into either the Catholic or Protestant category. Mormons deny they are Protestants. Their founder, Smith, declared all existing Christian denominations apostate and lacking authority to teach or to confer the priesthood. The Latter-day Saints frankly claim that their church alone represents the teaching authority of Jesus Christ.

Protestants themselves find it difficult to extend the term "Protestant" to a cult which denies every cardinal principle of the Reformation. The Mormons summarily dismiss the doctrines of total depravity, justification by faith alone, the sole sufficiency of the Bible, the priesthood of all believers. Only the reluctance of religious statisticians to set up a new LDS category keeps the Mormons in the Protestant column.

The followers of Smith have split into two major and several minor sects since Smith was assassinated in a Carthage, Illinois, jail. What has become the largest sect followed Brigham Young to the Great Salt Lake Valley and established itself in its intermountain sanctuary as the Church of Jesus Christ of Latter-day Saints, commonly known as the Mormon or LDS church.

A smaller group gathered around Smith's son and formed the Reorganized Church of Jesus Christ of Latter Day Saints with headquarters in Independence, Missouri. This church completed its organization in 1860. A pamphlet issued by the Reorganized branch states its complaints against the Utah Mormons: "Brigham Young headed the migration to Utah, where he introduced strange new doctrines to his followers: of plural gods, polygamy, and blood atonement, among others."

Another Reorganized booklet (*Hear Our Story*) comments, "The 'Reorganized' group has always denounced polygamy and the kindred evils promulgated in Utah as contrary to the teachings of the Bible and the Book of Mormon, as well as contrary to the example and teachings of Joseph Smith. No son or grandson of Joseph Smith has ever fellowshiped with the church in Utah."

The Reorganized sect builds no temples and allows its members to contribute to the church without necessarily tithing. Doctrinally this 155,000-member church stands somewhat closer to historic Christianity than the larger Utah cult. The Reorganized use a so-called "inspired" version of the Bible, a translation attempted by Smith and completed in 1833.

Mormonism as a religious system stands or falls on the validity of the revelation to Smith and the authenticity of the Book of Mormon. The official version tells us that the lad received a revelation from two divine personages in 1820 that all existing churches were apostate. He was to join none of them but was to reestablish the Church of Christ. Later an angel, Moroni, showed him the spot on a hillside in western New York where the last surviving general of an Indian nation had buried a set of golden plates. These plates told about the early inhabitants of this hemisphere, the visit of Christ after His resurrection, the wars and disasters which befell the Indians, and the church which Christ founded among them.

Smith sat behind a blanket stretched across a room in his cabin and dictated the book to a schoolmaster. The Prophet himself was unable to write. Since the plates were supposedly written in "Reformed Egyptian," the angel had provided the Prophet with magic spectacles known as the Urim and Thummin. By peeping through these Smith was able to decipher the text. Later the angel took back the plates and they have not been seen since.

As an historical romance the Book of Mormon makes fairly interesting reading. It includes large chunks of the King James version of the Bible and considers in some detail all the current theological debates of early nineteenth-century America: infant baptism, the Trinity, Freemasonry, the proper name of the Church, etc. The original plates were allegedly completed before A.D. 421.

Smith claimed that in 1829 John the Baptist appeared to him and restored the Aaronic priesthood. Later Peter, James, and John conferred the higher Melchizedek priesthood. Smith managed to persuade a farmer to mortgage his land to finance the publication of his book. He baptized the members of his family and some neighbors, sold the book door to door, and started what he called the Church of Christ.

During the next few years the Church established itself in Kirtland, Ohio, and in an outpost in Missouri. At this stage the cult put its emphasis on the imminent end of the world much as do Jehovah's Witnesses today. Smith warned his devotees to gather at Zion to escape the impending destruction. He located Zion at Independence, Missouri, which was also the site of the Garden of Eden.

Smith and his friend, Sidney Rigdon, an ex-Campbellite minister, became involved in the failure of a wildcat bank and were forced to flee Kirtland by night. They consolidated their position in Missouri until feuds with their Gentile neighbors, who feared their growing political power, abolitionist sentiment, and strange doctrines, led to bloodshed and eviction from the state.

In neighboring Illinois the Prophet directed the building of a model city on the Mississippi which he named Nauvoo. Meanwhile, the Prophet continued to receive a series of revelations including one in which God spelled out the financial arrangements for a Nauvoo boardinghouse: "And they shall not receive less than fifty dollars for a share of stock in that house, and they shall be permitted to receive fifteen thousand dollars from any one man for stock in that house." God also commanded that a house be built for his servant, Joseph Smith, Jr. (Sec. 41).

Smith set up an armed militia with himself in the uniform of a lieutenant general. He even ran for president of the United States and sent his missionaries around the country to seek votes. Nauvoo became the largest city in the state and operated under an unusually liberal charter. Its population reached 20,000.

Trouble brewed. Smith and a few of the top church officials had begun to take additional wives in Nauvoo and rumors of polygamy aroused the Gentiles in the area. One of Smith's cronies apostatized and denounced the Prophet and his sexual adventures. The opposition tried to publish a newspaper in Nauvoo but Smith's henchmen pied the type and destroyed the press.

In the ensuing disorders, Smith was arrested and taken into protective custody in Carthage, the center of anti-Mormon agitation. A mob of men masquerading as Indians stormed the jail and shot the 38-year-old Prophet and his brother Hyrum, the heir apparent. Fortunately for the stunned Saints, a remarkable leader named Brigham Young assumed Smith's mantle of leadership over the claims of several rivals. He organized the epic march to the West.

Other groups of Saints followed such self-proclaimed prophets as the mad King James Strang of Beaver Island. Rigdon tried to assert his authority but was repudiated and left for Pennsylvania and obscurity. Emma Smith, the Prophet's first and only legal wife, stayed in Nauvoo, married a Nauvoo tavern-keeper, and finally joined the Reorganized Church.

The invading Gentiles fired the handsome Mormon temple and took over what the retreating Saints could not load onto their wagons. Today a convent of Catholic Sisters has purchased some of the old Mormon property in Nauvoo, a sleepy river town.

Once the Saints reached the Salt Lake Valley they were free to set up a theocracy, openly practice polygamy, and develop their curious theological system. To their dismay they found their new land of Deseret incorporated into the hated United States shortly after their arrival; they had sought to leave the country which had persecuted them for so many years.

For the average Mormon convert the idea of polygamy was probably repugnant. Those who did take plural wives usually did so out of obedience to a divine command rather than out of lechery. Many of the plural wives were elderly women; sometimes a Mormon would marry a mother and daughter set. For most of the Saints the economic battle to support one wife and family was enough, let alone the support of multiple households.

The Book of Mormon clearly outlaws the practice of polygamy: "Wherefore, my brethren, hear me, and hearken to the word of the Lord: For there shall not be any man among you save it be one wife; and concubines he shall have none" (Jacob, Chap. 2, v. 27).

In Doctrine and Covenants, published in 1835, we read: "Inasmuch as this Church of Christ has been reproached with the crime of fornication and polygamy, we declare that we believe that one man should have one wife, and one woman one husband, except in case of death, when either is at liberty to marry again" (Sec. 101).

Brigham Young married 27 women but the 27th wife sued him for divorce and stumped the country to denounce polygamy. He fathered 56 children. His life long friend, Heber Kimball supported 45 wives. About 8 per cent of Mormon families were plural families during the period when polygamy was openly acknowledged.

Eastern editors, social reformers, and preachers raged against the scandal of polygamy on American soil and pressured Congress into passing a series of antipolygamy laws. The Church found its property confiscated, its members disfranchised, its leaders in jail or in hiding. Unable to fight the power of the federal government indefinitely, the elderly president of the church finally capitulated. The church renounced the active practice of plural marriage and said it would excommunicate Saints who contracted new plural marriages. In exchange Washington granted statehood to Utah. Some Saints set up separate households and continued to live with several wives; a few fled to Mexico with their families.

Polygamy remains a suspended doctrine. Not once have LDS church officials denied that the taking of plural wives was a divine command given to the Prophet or that if the law of the land were ever changed, the Church would not reintroduce polygamy. Mormons consider the laws against plural marriage to be violations of religious freedom.

Small groups of Mormon fundamentalists in Utah and Arizona continue to enter plural marriages and castigate the larger church for giving in to civil power. *Time* magazine comments: "What they practice openly, thousands of others throughout the West practice in secret" (Jan. 23, 1956).

Over the years up to 1870 the Mormons constructed an elaborate and secret temple ritual, based largely on Masonic models. Smith, Young, and the Nauvoo hierarchy of the church entered the Masonic lodge with enthusiasm and appropriated parts of the Masonic ritual for their temple rites. (Like polygamy, Freemasonry was condemned in the *Book of Mormon* as an invention of Satan.) Masonic-type aprons, symbols, passwords, and secret names have found their way into these rites which are closed to all Gentiles and lukewarm Mormons.

In their 12 temples the Mormons conduct four main rites: baptism for the dead, marriage for time and eternity, endowments, and sealing of parents and children. Mormons who wish to enter the portals of the temple must provide proof that they tithe their income, abstain from tobacco, liquor, coffee, and tea, and attend church with regularity. If they qualify, their local bishop (pastor) will give them a "recommend" which they can present at the temple.

In baptism of the dead the Saints undergo proxy baptism by immersion for their ancestors or prominent people in history who must receive the sacrament to advance in the afterlife. To trace their ancestors they prepare extensive genealogical records.

Christians marry "until death do them part." Mormons say they marry for time and eternity. They believe the family relationships continue forever. A Mormon who marries another Mormon or a Gentile in a ward chapel is married only for time. A loyal Mormon will prefer to marry another Mormon in a temple ceremony. Unless a man and wife (or wives) are thus properly sealed in the temple they can never hope to reach the state of godhead. If a Mormon couple first entered a marriage for time they may be sealed together with any children in a later temple rite.

Mormons receive their introduction into esoteric Mormonism in the endowment ceremony. Men and women enter wearing white garments and are bathed and anointed with oil. They don the long underwear which an observing Mormon wears throughout life and in which he or she is buried. The holy underwear is marked by three symbols to indicate that if the initiate should reveal the contents of the rite he will agree to have his legs cut off at the knee, his bowels removed, and his heart cut out. The initiates also wear white trousers or robe and girdle, a cloth cap, moccasins, and a green silk apron. They get a secret name used only in the church and watch playlets depicting points of Mormon doctrine. Anyone familiar with Masonic ritual will see dozens of parallels.

To this day Mormons are discouraged from joining the Masonic lodge and the Grand Lodge of Utah blackballs Mormon applicants. Smith and his cohorts were eventually expelled from the Illinois lodge for initiating Saints wholesale and turning the lodge into an arm of the Mormon church.

Practically every male Mormon over 12 in good standing belongs to some grade of the Mormon priesthood: teacher, priest, elder, seventy, high priest. Each Mormon gets a sense of belonging and the institution of the priesthood has become a strong cement in the Mormon community. Only a small number of church officials receive a salary; the Mormon bishop serves his congregation without pay while holding a secular job. The young missionaries who give two years of their lives on assignments around the world get no pay; their parents or Mormon businessmen furnish transportation, room, and board.

David O. McKay, 89, heads the church as president, assisted by two counselors and Twelve Apostles. Together they form a self-perpetuating body known as the Big 15. Local congregations are called wards and a number of wards in a given area form a stake with a president and two counselors. Wards are kept small and once

300 or so members join a particular ward the stake president will probably form a new ward.

The cult considers the Negro a member of a cursed race and therefore ineligible for the priesthood. Young explained, "Why are so many of the inhabitants of the Earth cursed with a skin of blackness? It comes in consequence of their fathers rejecting the power of the Holy Priesthood and the law of God." Mormons believe Negroes are descendants of Cain. On the other hand, the Saints traditionally display solicitude for the American Indians, descendants of the people of the *Book of Mormon*. The LDS church is now one of the largest in Hawaii and wins many converts among the Polynesians in other Pacific islands.

Mormonism furnishes a complete religious and social life to its members. Every ward schedules dances, parties, picnics, sports activities, as well as religious services and priesthood meetings. Welfare agencies care for unemployed or disabled Mormons. Mormon charity and social concern seem generally limited to the needs of fellow Mormons. Mormon families give up two meals on one Sunday a month and donate the cost of the missed meals to the church to help the needy.

The LDS church encourages large families and frowns on birth control for theological reasons. Divorces among those couples who marry in a temple are rare. The typical Mormon will be chaste, free from habits of drinking or smoking, eager to continue his education or give a college education to his children, industrious, and dedicated to his church.

Saddled with the preposterous fable about the golden plates and magic spectacles and guided through the years by amateur theologians, the Mormon church offers a theology compounded from elements of spiritualism, materialism, Freemasonry, Judaism, Swedenborgianism, Campbellism, Christianity, paganism, and sexual myth.

The current doctrine of the deity indicates that God the Father and Jesus Christ are two distinct flesh-and-bone (but not blood) personages. God the Father is a material being, a polygamist. The Holy Ghost has a spirit body. God the Father, an exalted and perfect man, resides near the planet "Kolob."

In the beginning three things existed: God, matter, and intelligence. God did not create matter but He "organized" it. He also procreated an immense number of souls whose destiny as future gods depends on a successful transition through the experience of human life. These spirits agree to forget their preexistence to be born as men. As men they advance to the state of godhead by repenting of their sins, receiving Mormon baptism and laying on of hands, becoming obedient to the priesthood. They may attain the highest celestial glory by going through the temple ceremony which seals a man and wife for eternity. An unmarried Mormon can never achieve this status and a male can clinch his chances by marrying not one but many women in the temple. After death the faithful Mormon may achieve godhead and get charge of his own planet and rule as this planet's god. "What man is now God once was; what God is now man may become," said Young.

God created Jesus and Lucifer. Lucifer promised to save men by depriving them of free will but God disagreed and sentenced him to hell. Mormons consider sexual intercourse to be the forbidden fruit of the Garden of Eden (in Missouri). But God also commanded Adam and Eve to increase and multiply. Adam in disobeying God and having intercourse with Eve chose the lesser of two evils.

Three grades in the afterlife are possible destinations of worthy people. Only temple-married Mormons will reach the celestial heaven and divinity. Lower-grade Mormons and unusually good Christians will live forever on the terrestrial plane presided over by Jesus. Garden-variety Gentiles will have to be content with the telestial plane and fraternization with ministering angels. Only a few murderers and apostates will go to perdition.

To go from door to door selling this weird brand of religion in twentieth-century America would put anyone to the test. The canny Mormons try to sugarcoat their theological hodgepodge until the prospective convert gets deeper into esoteric Mormonism. The dark-suited young men will simply introduce themselves as ministers or elders of the Church of Jesus Christ of Latter-day Saints which may mean nothing to an Indiana or New York housewife. They ask permission to offer a prayer for the welfare of the family. They may present a copy of the Articles of Faith drawn up at Nauvoo to camouflage the unorthodox doctrines of the young cult.

Outside of occasional contact with the ubiquitous Mormon missionaries the average Gentile probably thinks of Mormonism only in terms of Salt Lake City and its temple and tabernacle, ribald stories about polygamy, Mormon objections to coffee and tea. They may hear the Mormon Tabernacle Choir on TV singing a Bach Mass or Christmas hymn. They may know about the religious commitment of Ezra Taft Benson or George Romney.

Mormonism is activist, tidy, prosperous. It offers a sense of security and community to its members. The Saints promote higher education. Utah boasts more college graduates per capita than any other of the 50 states.

Many born Mormons or converts no doubt remain in the system because of its social cohesiveness not to say clannishness. To abandon the LDS church in many western communities would take more courage than to swallow the Smith fables and theological monstrosities. It would mean social ostracism and perhaps business boycott.

Why has Mormonism grown while so many other cults and prophets have been forgotten? We may enumerate the fascination of the *Book of Mormon*, the cohesive pressure of persecution, the value of martyrdom, the charismatic powers of Brigham Young, the rare opportunity to build the theocracy in the Rocky Mountains. In addition the LDS church remains one of the few non-Catholic bodies to condemn birth control; the Mormon birth rate of 33.3 per thousand compares to the national average of 24 per thousand. The death rate for Mormons is lower than that of Gentiles. An aggressive missionary program brings substantial numbers of converts and the small, intimate ward organization discourages backsliding and apostasy.

Mormonism will probably continue to grow despite its discredited archaeology, racism, and bizarre theology. To its adherents, both those in the Rocky Mountain area and in the Diaspora, it provides a satisfying way of life. Its amateur theologians accept its myths and prefer not to subject its basic beliefs to too careful a scrutiny.

CHAPTER 5

BAHA'ISM

This Offshoot of Islam Gains More
Attention Than Converts in America

———— • ————

When singer Vic Damone announced recently that he was leaving the Catholic Church to become a Baha'i most Catholics probably wondered what in the world a Baha'i could be. Many residents of the Chicago area have no doubt seen the gleaming white Baha'i temple on the shores of Lake Michigan in Wilmette but few know anything about the religion which inspired its construction.

Briefly, Baha'i is an offshoot of Islam bearing about the same relation to that faith as Mormonism does to orthodox Christianity. The cult demands the same unquestioned acceptance of its prophets and scriptures as Mormonism demands of Joseph Smith and his *Book of Mormon*. To Moslems the Baha'is are simply heretics.

A Moroccan court sentenced three Baha'is to death as heretics in 1962 and gave prison terms to six others. Islam is the state religion of Morocco. Baha'is in other countries protested the action and sought to bring the case before the United Nations commission on human rights.

Most of the world's two million Baha'is live in Persia where the faith originated about 100 years ago; another sizable group lives in India. The American branch of the Baha'i World Faith counts a tiny (about 10,000) constituency, a fairly extensive literature in English, one House of Worship, and a potential for growth which should not be underestimated.

Unity is the theme of the Baha'i movement. Baha'is preach the essential unity of all the major religions and the brotherhood of mankind. They plump for the United Nations, the international auxiliary language Esperanto, elimination of race prejudice, compulsory education, equal rights for women, a world court, the harmony of science and religion. The last Guardian of the Faith, who died of a heart attack in London, summarized the religious basis of the cult as follows:

> The fundamental principle enunciated by Baha'u'llah, the followers of His Faith firmly believe, is that religious truth is not absolute but relative, that Divine Revelation is a continuous and progressive process, that all the great religions of the world are divine in origin, that their basic principles are in complete harmony, that their aims and purposes are one and the same, that their teachings are but facets of one truth, that they differ only in the nonessential aspects of their doctrines, and that their missions represent successive stages in the spiritual evolution of human society.

On the surface the cult seems to offer modern man a progressive common-sense faith quite in harmony with many noble aspirations. Its creed might almost be taken over as the platform of a liberal political party. Esoteric Baha'ism, however, turns out to be considerably more dogmatic than appearance would indicate. Doctrines of its two Persian prophets must be accepted as divine and infallible. In its foreign versions it is frankly anti-Christian as well as anti-Islam. Membership involves obedience to a highly centralized spiritual authority and the cult can only be compared to the Mother Church of Christian Science in the zeal with which it censors, guards, and directs devotees and dogmas.

A tradition of the Shaykis sect of Shi'ih Islam concerned the appearance of a Messiah, the mysterious 12th Imman, similar to the Jewish belief. In 1844 a young Persian merchant, Mirza Ali-Muhammad, declared himself to be the Herald who, like John the Baptist, would prepare the way for the Messiah. (Pamphlets of the cult tell us this took place two hours and 11 minutes after sunset on May 22, 1844.) He persuaded most of the Shaykis to accept his claims. Hounded by the Islamic leaders the young man, who took the name of Bab (the Gate), was exiled, imprisoned, tortured, and finally executed in 1850. One of his mentally unbalanced disciples took a potshot at the Shah, which precipitated a wholesale massacre of more than 10,000 Babis.

The Babi who declared himself to be the Promised One, known to us as Baha'u'llah (the Glory of God), suffered the same persecution. An early follower of the Bab, whom he never met personally, Baha'u'llah succeeded in establishing his claim to prophethood in the face of about 25 rivals in the Babi movement. His half brother led a smaller group of Babis who rejected Baha'u'llah's claims and still await the Messiah.

Baha'u'llah spent more than 40 years in and out of prisons and died in a Turkish penal colony in Akka in 1892. In more than 100 volumes and tablets he elaborated his religious views. According to Baha'u'llah (the Blessed Perfection, as he was called), every age receives a Manifestation of God and a spiritual message suitable to its level of understanding. He acknowledged the authority of the earlier Manifestations — Abraham, Moses, Zoroaster, Jesus, Buddha, and Mohammed — but maintained that he had been appointed to be the prophet for the present age. A basic Baha'i belief asserts that all the major religions teach the same divine truths, perverted only by misinterpretation and the dogmas of later orthodoxies.

In a series of open letters to the world's rulers, Baha'u'llah urged the recognition of his claims. Among the recipients were the Pope, Queen Victoria, the Sultan, the American presidents, the Kaiser, the high priests of Zoroastrianism, and the leaders of the Shi'ih and Sunni branches of Islam.

When he died, the mantle of leadership fell on his eldest son, Abdul-Baha (the Servant of Baha). He also spent about 40 years in prison but was released by the Young Turks in 1908 and later toured Egypt, Europe, and the United States. He broke ground for the Wilmette temple in 1912 — it was not dedicated until 1953. He made his home in Haifa and was knighted by the British for his humanitarian work during World War I. After his death in 1921 his body was placed in a mausoleum on Mount Carmel; the cultists buried the body of the Bab in the same area after hiding his remains for 60 years. Abdul-Baha interpreted the writings of his father and is honored as one of the world's great religious figures by the Baha'is but he lacks the divine authority of the Bab and Baha'u'llah.

His grandson, Shoghi Effendi Rabbani, an Oxford student, succeeded to leadership. He continued the expansion and administrative organization of the cult until his death in 1957. In 1963 the Baha'is elected a nine-member Universal House of Justice as supreme legislative power. Haifa remains international headquarters; there the cult maintains a number of marble buildings and shrines.

Spiritual numerology fascinated Baha'u'llah and his devotees. For example, the number nine holds a special sacred significance. Baha'u'llah maintained that his new religion, the ninth, was built on the eight major world religions which preceded it; these he identified as Sabianism, Buddhism, Hinduism, Zoroastrianism, Judaism, Christianity, Mohammedanism, and Babism. Local spiritual assemblies receive recognition when they enroll nine members. They elect nine members of the National Spiritual Assembly at Wilmette. Nine of the 27 Hands of the Faith must live in Haifa. The Baha'i Houses of Worship must be built with nine sides, etc.

Designed by a French-Canadian convert, Louis Bourgeois, the Wilmette temple cost more than $2,600,000 and seats 1200 in the main auditorium. The exterior has been covered by a special precast stone which gives it a lacy appearance. The nine alcoves are decorated with sayings of Baha'u'llah; like the mosque, the Baha'i temple employs only geometric designs or Arabic script for decoration. The outside columns depict the chronology of the major religions by means of the ancient swastika, the Star of David, the Christian cross, the star and crescent of Islam, and finally the nine-pointed star of the Baha'i faith.

Like Islam, the Baha'i faith employs no professional clergy. Local congregations get together every 19 days for worship which consists of prayer, meditation, and scripture readings. Only solos and a capella singing are allowed. Each year Baha'is observe a 19-day fast patterned after the Moslem Ramadan. No food or drink is allowed between sunrise and sunset. Baha'is follow a calendar of 19 months of 19 days with New Year's falling on March 21.

Baha'is, unlike their Moslem cousins, forbid polygamy. Marriages may be entered into only with the written consent of all living parents. A one-year trial separation must precede divorce. The cult forbids liquor, tobacco, and narcotics. It recommends prescribed short prayers such as "Ya Baha'u'l-Abha" (Oh Glory, the most Glorious) which, if repeated 95 times a day, is supposed to guarantee peace of soul to the believer.

Of course, the cult denies the divinity of Christ. Our Lord becomes simply one of a series of Manifestations of God or prophets. Baha'u'llah lifted the Islamic dispensation just as Islam replaced Christianity at an earlier date, according to the cult. Abdul-Baha called the Christian Eucharist an "absolute fantasy."

Essentially the Baha'is are agnostics who deny that God can be known by man. They deny original sin, the reality of sin and evil, the existence of hell. They teach that the universe is without a beginning or creation; it is rather a "perpetual emanation from the Great First Cause." After death the spirit progresses to a state of perfection. They do not hesitate to incorporate into their worship the scriptures of other religions: the Old and New Testaments, the Koran, the Vedas, etc. Baha'ism has been called the syncretic religion par excellence.

Most Baha'is outside the Chicago area meet in private homes and hotel rooms. The cult claims members in 1300 American communities and reports 40 new congregations launched during 1959. The Wilmette temple remains the only permanent House of Worship in this hemisphere. The immediate goal is to erect such temples on each continent and eventually in every large city in the world. A home for the aged has recently been opened near the Wilmette temple and is the first of a complex of educational and philanthropic institutions to be built around each temple: a hospital, orphanage, science institute, and college.

The cult enlists the services of a number of self-supporting missionaries known as Pioneers who organize local assemblies wherever they are sent. Baha'is conduct summer schools at Eliot, Maine; Geyserville, California; and Davidson, Michigan. The national body places ads in dozens of newspapers and magazines and tries to interest some of the 100,000 annual visitors to Wilmette in its teachings. It reaps publicity in scores of cities by sponsoring World Religion Day on the third Sunday of January.

Probably the best known converts were Queen Marie of Rumania and the late film star Carole Lombard. Like Christian Science, it draws its adherents from the distaff side in this country. The cult's heavily Arabic and exotic flavor probably repels some inquirers, but its emphasis on racial equality has won some Negro converts.

During the past decade the number of Baha'i communities has increased from 2,000 to 13,000 although many such groups are tiny. About 450 American missionaries for the faith try to win converts overseas. These Pioneers serve without pay. More than 6,000 Baha'is from 70 countries attended the first Baha'i world congress in London in 1963.

Baha'is do not seem to be discouraged by the relatively slow progress of their religion, which they are sure will supplant all existing religions. They point out that despite intense persecution and periodic pogroms in Persia it has spread to more than 240 nations, territories, and islands. Like Marxists, the Baha'is go ahead confident that the world is moving inexorably toward unity which is the central theme of their new religion. The time will come, they believe, when the people of the world will look in desperation to Baha'u'llah for answers to the problems caused by such things as nationalism, race prejudice, and superstition.

They are having some difficulty at the moment holding all the followers of Baha'u'llah in one organization. A splinter group has broken away to form the New History Foundation, which sponsors a youth movement called the Caravan of East and West. Another branch follows Charles Mason Remey, an American who has proclaimed himself the new Guardian of the Faith.

Catering to a desire for novelty and mysticism, a relaxed sexual code, a frank racial equality, many cults such as Baha'i will probably attract a growing number of Americans searching for religious status outside the Christian community.

CHAPTER 6

SPIRITUALISM

The Living Often Attempt to Communicate With the Dead

———— • ————

Many reasons have impelled men and women to try to reach their dead loved ones: a need for personal assurance of their own immortality, guilt feelings which may be assuaged by words from the grave, curiosity, fear of the harm which spirits can inflict on the survivors, a belief that the spirits can heal and help the living. As a result we see that Spiritualism or Spiritism has been practiced by all peoples as far back as recorded history.

In some areas, such as Brazil and Haiti, Spiritualism mixed with Christianity presents a genuine threat to the Church. In the United States the number of active Spiritualists is small, perhaps 175,000, although many others, usually women, attend seances and Spiritualist services occasionally.

In this country Spiritualism takes on a Christian flavor. Jesus Christ is considered a great medium. The Annunciation was a message from the spirit world; the Transfiguration was a materialization of Moses and Elias; and the Resurrection was evidence of life beyond the grave.

American Spiritualists may baptize members and a few Spiritualist churches even hold communion services. Spiritualist mediums can obtain ministerial ordination which allows them to perform marriages and burials and which incidentally makes prosecution for fraud and deception extremely difficult.

What we know as modern Spiritualism began in the 1840's in New York. Of course, many years before this, Swedenborg had claimed to be able to communicate with the inhabitants of the spirit world. People held a general belief in spirits and haunted houses.

The "Poughkeepsie seer," Andrew Jackson Davis, published his book *Nature's Divine Revelations* in 1847, and would later provide the terminology and theoretical foundation for Spiritualism. What set off the modern interest in Spiritualism was the report of two young girls of Hydeville, New York, that they had heard mysterious raps and knocks in their home. March 31, 1848, is considered the birth date of modern Spiritualism. On this date one of the little girls asked the spirit rapper, "Here, Mr. Splitfoot, do as I do." The spirit responded and the girls and the spirit began to communicate through a code of knocks.

The Fox sisters, Margaret and Kate, managed to convince many visitors that these signals were genuine. They went on tour and gave demonstrations of these manifestations in public auditoriums.

Americans flocked to seances and within a few years thousands of mediums were active in the larger cities. The movement interested such people as James Fenimore Cooper, Daniel Webster, Harriet Beecher Stowe, William Cullen Bryant, Horace Greeley, and Hamlin Garland. In England Spiritualism was fostered by Sir Oliver Lodge, the scientist, and Arthur Conan Doyle, the creator of Sherlock Holmes. Even in more recent years the prime minister of Canada, Mackenzie King, was a convinced Spiritualist.

Both Fox sisters became alcoholics and in 1888 Margaret startled the Spiritualist world by confessing that she had made the signals by adroit toe snapping. She joined the Catholic Church for a while but went back to the profession of mediumship.

Spiritualism had almost died out by the start of the twentieth century but was revived by World War I. Parents and wives of soldiers killed on the battlefields of Europe began to visit mediums who promised to deliver messages from the other world. Sir Oliver Lodge published a famous book entitled *Raymond*, which purported to be conversations with his dead son.

Mediums use various methods to communicate with the spirits and to demonstrate their psychic powers. The most common method is the platform demonstration in which the medium simply relays messages supposedly received from the spirit. In many cases these messages are received from a "control" spirit rather than from the spirit itself. The control may often be an American Indian since Spiritualists believe the Indians possess especially sensitive powers of communication.

The average seance is attended by only 20 or 25 people. The medium, usually a woman, sits in the darkened room and goes into a trance before she begins to deliver messages to the circle of devotees.

The medium may also demonstrate other spirit manifestations. The voice of the dead person may emanate from a trumpet suspended in the air; a milky substance known as ectoplasm may be seen to come from the medium's mouth and take a human shape; music, voices, perfume, or cool breezes may drift from a cabinet in which the medium is bound, gagged, and seated; objects may float around the room and flashes and pinpoints of light may illuminate the seance room. Slate writing, spirit photography, healing, automatic writing, and the Ouija board may be used by the Spiritualist medium.

Master magician Harry Houdini maintained he could duplicate any of these effects by stage magic. He attended hundreds of seances and offered a substantial reward to any medium who could outwit him but no one collected the prize.

Intelligent people who dabble in Spiritualism are often disillusioned by the banal answers given by the spirits. The information they impart in the seance is trivial and commonplace. Spiritualist enthusiasts explain that the only spirits who are allowed to get in touch with the living are those living on one of the lower spirit planes, Summerland. At this stage they have made little progress in spiritual development and so have little to reveal.

Traditional Spiritualist theology describes seven levels in the hereafter. The first level begins about 300 miles above the earth and the last extends to about 18,000 miles. The two low levels serve as spirit home for the unrepentant wicked people; no one is so bad as to deserve an eternal hell, say the Spiritualists.

Most people end up in the third level, Summerland. This spirit level corresponds to earthly existence. Summerland's residents wear clothing, live in houses, own pets, marry their soul mates. The fourth level is for philosophers, the fifth for contemplatives, the sixth is known as the love sphere, and the seventh is the Christ sphere.

Spiritualism is devoid of any ethical content or social outreach. The spirits seem content with ordinary creature comforts and the people attending the seances are typically wrapped up in themselves and their dead relatives. God plays a minor role in Spiritualism although most American Spiritualists would call themselves theists and Christians.

How much fraud is prevalent in Spiritualism today is hard to determine. Some Spiritualists admit that perhaps as many as nine out of ten mediums are frauds; they are content to believe that the tenth medium is genuine. These people want a demonstration of immortality rather than the assurance of the Bible or the Church.

The Catholic Church has always warned the faithful against entanglement in Spiritualism. Books advocating Spiritualism are condemned by canon law and since 1917 Catholics have been forbidden to attend seances even as spectators. Of course, this prohibition does not extend to the scientific investigation of phenomena such as that carried on by the Society for Psychic Research.

Many Spiritualist congregations consist of the personal following of a particular medium. Seances and worship services are held in hired halls or hotel rooms. Congregations are more or less autonomous but may join together in loosely organized federations.

Three national Spiritualist associations are fairly well established. The National Spiritualist Association, organized in 1893, remains the leading body. It prescribes rituals for worship, baptism, and funerals and ordains clergymen, lecturers, and mediums. The NSA operates the Morris Pratt Institute in Wisconsin, a two-year school which trains aspiring Spiritualist ministers and mediums. The International General Assembly of Spiritualists holds an annual meeting and has its headquarters in Norfolk, Virginia. The National Spiritual Alliances of the United States of America holds its annual convention at Lake Pleasant, Massachusetts.

Summer Spiritualist camps are held at Lily Dale, New York, and at Chesterfield, Indiana. At the Chesterfield camp, classes and seances are held every day from the end of June to around the middle of August. At the 1962 camp 21 staff mediums and several visiting mediums assisted at the daily seances. Facilities at the camp include an art gallery which features relics of the Fox sisters and other pioneer mediums; a Garden of Prayer with a life-size statue of Jesus; another monument to an American Indian; a Church in the Wildwood where regular Sunday services are scheduled; a new cafeteria; a bookstore; and a Congress of Religions shrine with busts of the founders of the world religions.

Time magazine estimates more than 10 million Spiritualists in Brazil. The Brazilian Spiritual Foundation, founded 77 years ago, claims 3600 centers. On New Year's Eve more than 600,000 people have participated in outdoor seances on the beaches near Rio de Janeiro. To counteract the growth of Spiritualism the Marist Brothers in Rio de Janeiro have studied magic and put on public shows to expose the deception of the native mediums.

In France and Italy the Spiritualists subscribe to the theories of Allan Kardec, which include a belief in reincarnation. The *Sunday Times* for June 24, 1960, estimated a membership of about 250,000 in 1000 Spiritualist churches in England. The best known contemporary English Spiritualist is Lord Dowding, former chief of the Royal Air Force.

Membership in American Spiritualist churches is predominately female although men sometimes hold the top offices in national associations. Many Spiritualist churches are fly-by-night operations. Rarely does a Spiritualist attend one particular church; she is more likely to shop around visiting a number of mediums. It is reasonable to assume that there are two or three Spiritualists to every one who belongs to a recognized Spiritualist church.

Spiritualism does emphasize the preparatory character of human life and in this it differs from many liberal Protestant bodies which gloss over the fact of death. Its total self-centeredness and lack of theological depth deprive Spiritualism of any significant influence on American religious life. Its infestation by mountebanks and frauds discourages all but the most committed.

As G. K. Chesterton asked, "Do you expect to hear the voice of God calling from a coal cellar?"

CHAPTER 7

SEVENTH-DAY ADVENTISM

Adventists Prepare for World's End and Observe Strict Sabbath

Seldom do we pick up our daily newspaper without reading about new wars and rumors of war, earthquakes, famines, Russian missile gains, fires, labor troubles, and a score of other disasters and dangers. To more than 1,000,000 people around the world these news stories only prove what they have been preaching for almost 100 years: the end of the world is near and we are living in the last days before the Second Coming. They are Seventh-day Adventists.

They do not stand alone in this conviction. Jehovah's Witnesses trace their beginning to Pastor Russell's early encounter with an Adventist preacher. Joseph Smith excited his Mormon followers into a sense of urgency about the last things and they applied the term *Latter-day* Saints to themselves. The Adventist family itself embraces several minor sects as well as the main Seventh-day branch.

We would be mistaken if we imagined that the Seventh-day Adventists differed from other Protestants only in their emphasis on the end of the world and their observance of Saturday instead of Sunday. Several other distinctive beliefs set the Adventists apart from the Baptists and Methodists and Presbyterians who form the majority of United States Protestants.

For example, the Adventists attach a special importance to the writings of Mrs. Ellen G. White who, they believe, possessed the spirit of prophecy. Mrs. White (1827–1915) holds a position in the sect somewhat comparable to that of Mary Baker Eddy in Christian Science or Madame Blavatsky in Theosophy.

Another Adventist position not shared by other Protestants is commonly referred to as the doctrine of soul sleep. The SDA sect teaches that man is not immortal. After death he falls into a sleep from which he may be raised at the resurrection. The wicked do not suffer punishment in an eternal hell but are destroyed, annihilated.

On the level of personal morals the Adventists continue to enforce a strict Puritanism which forbids the use of liquor, tobacco, coffee and tea, cosmetics. Members are discouraged from attending the theater, movies, or dances, playing cards, or joining a lodge. Total abstinence becomes a test of Christian living.

Beyond these injunctions which characterize many lower-class Holiness sects as well, the SDA church imposes Old Testament laws against the eating of meat of "unclean" animals such as pork or shrimp. Adventists are "kosher" Christians. In fact most Adventists, for religious and health reasons eat no meat at all and avoid seasoning such as pepper.

To support a far-flung educational, missionary, health, and publishing effort the church expects members to contribute what amounts to a double tithe or 20 percent of their incomes. Per capita giving by the Adventists puts the larger, older Protestant denominations to shame. In a recent year the average Adventist gave $203 a year to the church and another $35 to the missions. This is per member, not per family. In comparison the average Methodist gave $48 and $1.74 to the missions and the upper-class Protestant Episcopal Church reported an average contribution of $53.48 with an extra $1.20 for mission work.

Since the 1860's the sect has emphasized health and medical care to a far greater extent than other fundamentalist churches. The famous Battle Creek sanitarium was founded by the church but has since cut church ties. The SDA church still operates 23 hospitals in the United States and Canada and many more overseas. An Adventist, Kellogg, invented corn flakes as a health food. Thousands of Adventist doctors, dentists, and nurses got their training at the Adventist College of Medical Evangelists in Loma Linda, California. It holds a Class A rating.

The church attempts to provide a religious education for all its young people from kindergarten to college. The SDA church sponsors the largest Protestant parochial school system outside the Lutherans and tries to set up a school whenever six or more pupils can be assembled. Adventists control 11 liberal arts colleges, two junior colleges, a seminary, and a medical school in this country. Studies indicate that the Adventists count three times as many college graduates in their ranks as the general population.

Only the 10 million member Methodist Church assigns more foreign missionaries — 1500 — than the Seventh-day Adventists whose 317,000 United States adherents support 1400 overseas missionaries. Many whole islands in the Pacific have been converted to Adventism, such as Pitcairn Island of *Mutiny on the Bounty* fame. South America has become the sect's principal mission field. Around the world the SDA church employs 46,000 people — about one Adventist in 19 works for the church.

To trace the beginnings of this aggressive sect we must go back to the early decades of the nineteenth century. A number of Protestant clergymen in Europe had become excited about the Second Coming and this enthusiasm reached American shores. A Baptist lay preacher and 1812 war veteran, William Miller, pondered this question and using the Bible as a mathematical equation calculated that the end of the world would come in 1843. When 1843 drew to a close he fixed a second date on October 22, 1844, and when the world continued intact on October 23, the movement he fathered fell to pieces.

A handful of Adventists clung to Miller's original calculations and devised allegorical and invisible interpretations of the fiasco. One of these groups added the doctrines of the Saturday Sabbath and the special inspiration of Mrs. White to form what we know as Seventh-day Adventism. Miller himself never sanctioned these developments.

Mrs. White received her visions in a trancelike state which could last from 15 minutes to three hours during which she seemed to survive without breathing. Her eyesight would not return for several hours after she came out of a trance.

In one of her visions the Adventist prophetess claimed that she was shown the Ten Commandments in stone tablets with a special halo around the Fourth (Catholic Third) Commandment. She declared that failure to observe Saturday marked one with the mark of the beast. The Roman pope, the anti-Christ, had changed the Christian observance to Sunday and incurred God's holy wrath.

Adventists observe the Jewish Sabbath beginning at sundown Friday night. They abstain from cooking and unnecessary work, spend Saturday morning in church, and read the Bible and church literature for the rest of the day. Adventists close their stores and offices on Saturday as do Orthodox Jews. Logically enough, Adventists part company with other fundamentalists when the latter promote Sunday Blue Laws.

Adult candidates for baptism agree to abstain from liquor and tobacco and "unclean" foods, to tithe their income, to consider the SDA church the "remnant" church in contrast to the apostate churches of Christendom. In the Lord's Supper, Adventists use grape juice and observe a foot-washing ceremony before communion.

Adventists consider themselves conscientious cooperators as far as military service is concerned. The church has established camps which train Adventist young men for medical and noncombat duties. An Adventist corporal won the Congressional Medal of Honor for heroism on Okinawa during World War II.

Today the SDA denomination counts 1,155,000 adult members while 1,500,000 attend Adventist Sabbath schools. The sect runs 44 publishing houses and prints tracts and books in almost 200 languages. Their literary output is high if undistinguished: 385 magazines and 60 books a year flow from Adventist pens and presses. The "Voice of Prophecy" program reaches people in 65 languages over 860 radio stations, and their "Faith for Today" TV program is carried on 153 stations in the United States alone. The Adventists have a penchant for disguising the sponsorship of their broadcasts, periodicals, and public lectures, a practice which antagonizes other Protestants.

Mrs. White once wrote, "We should not go out of the way to make hard thrusts at the Catholics. Among the Catholics there are many who are most conscientious Christians who walk in all the light that shines upon them, and God will work in their behalf." Nevertheless Adventist propagandists usually dispense a rather strong dose of anti-Catholicism. The sect brands the pope the anti-Christ and employs childish numerical puzzles to buttress their views. They promote an extravagant position on separation of Church and State which no Catholics and few Protestants would support.

To a Catholic the theological contortions of the Adventists are understandable once you reject the proper role of tradition and substitute the trance-visions of Mrs. White for the teaching authority of the Church.

CHAPTER 8

NEW THOUGHT

This First Cousin of Christian Science
Seeks Health and Prosperity

———— • ————

Dozens of independent congregations and small denominations draw their inspiration from what is generally called the New Thought movement. New Thought is a point of view, a religious approach which is shared by churches with such titles as the Institute of Religious Science, Divine Science, the Unity Church of Truth, the Metaphysical School of Health, and many more.

The yellow pages in the telephone book and the Saturday church ads in most large cities list many such churches. Their congregations are likely to be small and predominantly female and most of the ministers are also women.

Although their outlook is similar to that of Christian Science, New Thought people consider the Mother Church to be a spiritual dictatorship. New Thought believers affirm the reality of matter but insist that mind can conquer matter. They tolerate physicians and medicine. Another closely related group is the Unity School of Christianity which at one time actually belonged to the international New Thought Alliance.

New Thought grew out of the New England of the middle nineteenth century. Some consider Ralph Waldo Emerson to be the spiritual father of the movement although the actual founder was the hypnotist and mental healer of Portland, Maine — Phineas P. Quimby.

The New England philosophers such as Emerson, Theodore Parker, Thoreau, and William Ellery Channing revolted against the official Calvinism of the day. Man, rather than depraved, was essentially good and given freedom, his mind could accomplish more than he had ever dreamed. Oriental religious thought influenced many of these American philosophers and brought with it ideas of pantheism.

In such soil the seed planted by Quimby grew. Born in 1802, he became a clockmaker by trade and dabbled in hypnotism. In some of his experiments he saw that hypnotism could be used to heal human ailments and he devised a theory that all healing lay in the mind rather than in medicine.

His fame as a healer spread and one of his patients was a Mrs. Patterson who has become better known to the world as Mary Baker Eddy. He was in the habit of allowing some of his clients to study his notes which were eventually compiled and published as the Quimby Manuscripts. Critics of Mrs. Eddy maintain that she appropriated large chunks of Quimby's thoughts for her own book *Science and Health*. She did get into print first since the Quimby Manuscripts were kept by his son for many years and only published after Christian Science was well launched.

Quimby taught that disease was not real; it was only a mental error. To cure the disease the sufferer must be convinced that he has accepted a false belief. He thought he had discovered the secret by which Jesus had performed His healings. These were not miracles, Quimby said, but simply the application of natural forces which others could apply as well.

Quimby died in 1866 without organizing a church or society to carry on his teachings. Two followers, Warren Felt Evans, a Swedenborgian clergyman, and Julius Dresser did the actual work of organizing the first New Thought movement.

New Thought groups grew up around the country without any central authority to establish an official doctrine. In contrast, the Christian Science movement was firmly under the hand of Mrs. Eddy. She wrote the official texts, censored lectures, exposed heresy, dismissed rivals and schismatics.

Groups of New Thought devotees got together as early as 1894 and conventions were held in major American cities. In 1914 these groups formed the International New Thought Alliance. Branches had sprung up in England, Europe, South Africa, Australia, and elsewhere.

In 1917 the Alliance adopted the following Declaration of Principles which still serves as the best description of New Thought beliefs:

We affirm the freedom of each soul as to choice and as to belief, and would not, by the adoption of any declaration of principles, limit such freedom. The essence of the New Thought is Truth, and each individual must be loyal to the Truth he sees. The windows of his soul must be kept open at each moment for the higher light, and his mind must be always hospitable to each new inspiration.

We affirm the Good. This is supreme, universal and everlasting. Man is made in the image of the Good, and evil and pain are but the tests and correctives that appear when his thought does not reflect the full glory of this image.

We affirm health, which is man's divine inheritance. Man's body is his holy temple. Every function of it, every cell of it, is intelligent, and is shaped, ruled, repaired, and controlled by mind. He whose body is full of light is full of health. Spiritual healing has existed among all races in all times. It has now become a part of the higher science and art of living the life more abundant.

We affirm the divine supply. He who serves God and man in the full understanding of the law of compensation shall not lack. Within us are unused resources of energy and power. He who lives with his whole being, and thus expresses fullness, shall reap fullness in return. He who gives himself, he who knows and acts in his highest knowledge, he who trusts in the divine return, has learned the law of success.

We affirm the teaching of Christ that the Kingdom of Heaven is within us, that we are one with the Father, that we should not judge, that we should love one another, that we should heal the sick, that we should return good for evil, that we should minister to others, and that we should be perfect even as our Father in Heaven is perfect. These are not only ideals, but practical, every-day working principles.

We affirm the new thought of God as Universal Love, Life, Truth and Joy, in whom we live, move, and have our being, and by whom we are held together; that His mind is our mind now, that realizing our oneness with Him means love, truth, peace, health and plenty, not only in our own lives but in the giving out of these fruits of the Spirit to others.

We affirm these things, not as a profession, but practice, not on one day of the week, but in every hour and minute of every day, sleeping and waking, not in the ministry of a few, but in a service that includes the democracy of all, not in words alone, but in the innermost thoughts of the heart expressed in living the life. "By their fruits ye shall know them."

We affirm Heaven here and now, the life everlasting that becomes conscious immortality, the communion of mind with mind throughout the universe of thoughts, the nothingness of all error and negation, including death, the variety in unity that produces the individual expressions of the One-Life, and the quickened realization of the indwelling God in each soul that is making a new heaven and a new earth.

We affirm that the universe is spiritual and we are spiritual beings. This is the Christ message to the twentieth century, and it is a message not so much of words as of works. To attain this, however, we must be clean, honest and trustworthy and uphold the Jesus Christ standards as taught in the Four Gospels. We now have the golden opportunity to form a real Christ movement. Let us build our house upon this rock, and nothing can prevail against it. This is the vision and mission of the Alliance.

New Thought differs from orthodox Christianity in many ways. It rejects the traditional concepts of heaven and hell as places of reward and punishment. Heaven is here and now. Some New Thoughters, such as those in Unity, believe in reincarnation.

The Trinity, original sin, and the redemptive work of Christ are ignored or denied. The New Thought concept of God is frankly pantheistic. Ernest Holmes, probably the best known New Thought writer, has said, "Every man is an incarnation of God; anyone who recognizes this and lives in conscious and harmonious union with Spirit, automatically becomes Christ." New Thought devotees grant no special inspiration to the Christian Bible and when they do use the Bible they are likely to interpret it allegorically or symbolically.

A number of people interested in New Thought retain membership in other Protestant denominations. New Thought, unlike Christian Science, allows such dual allegiance.

New Thought emphasizes the individual — his health, happiness, financial success. As a movement, New Thought does not engage in charitable work or operate institutions for the aged, orphaned, or sick. New Thoughters are much more likely to be too wrapped up in their own personalities to give much thought to the victims of "mental errors."

More than 1800 delegates attended a recent Alliance convention in Washington, D. C., dedicated to "Peace, Poise, Power, and Plenty." The Rev. Sarah Solada of the First Church of Understanding in Detroit told her audience to clutch a dollar bill while she intoned: "You want to love money so the next person who touches it will feel your love vibrating. You blessed money go out and do the work I intend you should do. Then return back to me that I may send more out again to do God's work."

Dr. Paul Martin Brunet of Science of Mind urged New Thoughters to affirm: "I am always where there is plenty of money." He explained that New Thoughters "want happy, vibrant, abundant money."

Sermons on healing also inspired the delegates. Dr. Ruth E. Chew outlined her "diet of joy." She asked everyone to repeat after her: "I am filled with joy; joy, gladness, and delight make everything all right." She claimed her joy diet could heal any ailment including TB and cancer.

The influence of New Thought is hard to measure; it is often disguised. Christians who could not define New Thought may have read Ralph Waldo Trine's *In Tune with the Infinite* which has sold over one million copies, subscribed to the attractive publications issued by the Unity School of Christianity, or even heard Emmet Fox preach to overflow crowds at Carnegie Hall. They may never know that all these books, magazines, and sermons are New Thought in content.

By any criteria New Thought continues to influence millions of Americans, even many who are active in other churches. The thousands who belong to New Thought-affiliated congregations are but the top of the iceberg.

CHRISTIAN SCIENCE

Mary Baker Eddy "Discovers"
Divine Principles of Healing

———— • ————

A public school teacher in California signs a statement every year that she is in perfect health and refuses to submit to a medical examination; she meets dozens of pupils in her classes and has an advanced case of tuberculosis.

Dentists and public health officials urge fluoridation of the city water supply to help cut down cavities among children. A group of citizens begins a propaganda campaign to halt the fluoridation project.

A youngster is struck down by a hit-and-run driver but his parents refuse all medical aid and hospitalization.

The California teacher, the members of the citizens' group, and the little boy's parents belong to the Church of Christ, Scientist. As Christian Scientists, they follow the religious system of a frail, thrice-married lady, Mary Baker Eddy.

Christian Scientists deny the reality of sin, sickness, and death. These are but phantoms of the human mind. Recently a writer for the cult declared that a Christian Scientist with the proper faith could have stood under the exploding atomic bomb at Hiroshima and escaped unharmed.

God is All, believe the Christian Scientists, and everything He created is good. If there seems to be disease and death and evil, they must be illusions of mortal mind. Men and women can free themselves from any sickness or injury by applying the "scientific" principles of Christian Science. Christ Himself performed His healings by simply applying the principles of divine law; there was nothing supernatural about these miracles.

Obviously Christian Science is a difficult religion to live by. Its estimated 350,000 adherents in the United States refuse the services of a physician but employ a dentist, obstetrician, and optometrist. They deny the reality of matter but seem as concerned as any of us with food, clothing, and shelter. They insist that Christian Science can overcome death itself, but their own leader died in 1910 and they too must eventually engage the service of the embalmer.

By any standards the woman who founded this strange cult must be considered a remarkable figure in the annals of religious history. Despite the relative successes of the Fox sisters (Spiritualism), Madame Blavatsky (Theosophy), and Aimee Semple McPherson, Mrs. Eddy remains the only woman to found a major religious movement.

At 50 Mrs. Eddy was an apparent failure, a widow with no real friends and no real home except boardinghouses. By the time she died of pneumonia at 89 she had amassed a fortune of three million dollars and was revered by 100,000 followers as their Leader and Mother.

Born in New Hampshire in 1821, she spent a rather unhappy childhood. She heard voices and was subject to fits of hysteria. At 22 she married a bricklayer but within a year he had died of yellow fever in South Carolina. She returned home to bear his son.

This tragedy aggravated her nervous condition and she turned for relief to spiritualism, homeopathy, and hypnosis. Friends took care of her baby and eventually he went with them to live in Minnesota. She tried marriage again. This time her choice was a philandering itinerant dentist, Dr. Daniel Patterson. He made the awkward mistake of wandering onto a Civil War battlefield and being captured by the Confederates. He spent two years in a POW camp.

Meanwhile Mrs. Patterson had heard of a marvelous healer in Portland by the name of Dr. Phineas P. Quimby. He scorned drugs and relied on hypnotism or mesmerism as it was called. His healing system was explained in a 10-volume work which he entitled *Science of Health*. Mrs. Patterson became his devoted pupil and patient and when Quimby died in 1866 she penned an effusive eulogy for the press.

Quimby had explained:

> My practice is unlike all medical practice. I give no medicine, and make no outward applications. I tell the patient his troubles, and what he thinks is his disease, and my explanation is the cure. If I succeed in correcting his errors, I change the fluids of the system, and establish the patient in health. The truth is the cure.

Later Mrs. Eddy denied her indebtedness to Quimby. In her textbook she declared, "No human pen or tongue taught me the science contained in the book." The average Christian Scientist considers her writings inspired by God.

"The Fall at Lynn," just one month after Quimby's demise, is regarded by Scientists as the date of the discovery of Christian Science. According to Mrs. Patterson's account she was returning home from a ladies-aid meeting when she slipped and fell. She maintained, and the attending physician denied, that she was told she would never walk again. Trusting in God she picked up her Bible, read several passages, and got out of bed. Her friends were astonished that she could once again get around, she reported.

Now she devoted every spare minute to writing her book which both she and her disciples considered inspired. Her husband, back from the wars, deserted his neurasthenic wife, gave up dentistry, and died a pauper in 1896. Meanwhile Mary went on with her engrossing work.

For years she labored over her book, handicapped by her ignorance of spelling and grammar but aided by the possession of certain notes and manuscripts of the late Dr. Quimby. She had also begun to practice faith healing and offered a series of 12 lessons for $300 which was about half a year's wages for the Lynn, Massachusetts, shoe workers who comprised her classes.

The book, *Science and Health*, appeared in 1875 and subsequently went through a number of revisions and editings. A section called "With Key to the Scriptures" was added which gave an allegorical interpretation of Genesis and the Book of Revelation.

Mary's final marriage was to a sewing-machine agent, Asa Gilbert

Eddy. When he died a few years later she told the newspaper reporters that he had been murdered by arsenic "mentally administered." The post mortem, however, disclosed a diseased heart.

Just as the scientific application of divine law could heal disease and repair injury, Mrs. Eddy reasoned that evil people could employ the same principles in reverse to inflict harm. This revival of witchcraft or voodoo she labeled Malicious Animal Magnetism, MAM. Her dread of MAM was to torment the poor woman and make her last days a hell on earth. She surrounded herself with a corps of devoted followers whose duty it was to ward off the evil influence of MAM. She particularly feared that the Catholic Church was trying to poison her mentally. At one time the cult's publications carried not only testimonials of healings but accounts of the workings of MAM. This feature has been quietly dropped and the whole question of MAM has become somewhat of an embarrassment to modern Christian Scientists.

She started a school at Boston called the Massachusetts Metaphysical College and in the eight years of its operation approximately 4000 students paid $1,200,000 in tuition. She was the entire faculty. She had also ordained herself a minister of the gospel in 1881 and was now known as "Rev."

When she was 68 she legally adopted a doctor who had worked with her at the college. Her natural son reappeared later in her career and threatened to take his mother to court as a mental incompetent. This suit was settled out of court, but Mrs. Eddy found herself embroiled in an exhausting series of litigations in her efforts to collect a 10 percent royalty on the healing fees of her students.

With considerable ingenuity and courage she set about to consolidate her position as head of the church. She dissolved the original Christian Science organization, ousted all pastors, and installed her book and the Bible as impersonal "pastors" of all branch churches.

By the time she completed her reorganization Christian Science consisted of one Mother Church in Boston. Local churches then as now were simply buildings where absentee members of the Boston congregation could meet to hear scripture and *Science and Health* readings, sing hymns, and deliver testimonials. Two lay readers served rotating three-year terms and directed the worship service according to a strict schedule sent from Boston headquarters. They did no preaching nor were they empowered to preside at baptisms, marriages, or funerals. To this day Chrisitan Scientists wishing to marry must find a judge or an obliging Protestant minister to perform the ceremony.

Lecturers were required to submit their speeches for detailed approval by Boston and the rules forbade any discussion period after the annual public lectures. Only Mrs. Eddy's own writings or authorized Christian Science publications were available in church-operated reading rooms.

The possibility of a personable preacher threatening Mrs. Eddy's hold on the church was eliminated by the rotating reader system. Conferences and regional meetings were banned, which discouraged organized revolts. Everything depended on the approval of Boston and Mrs. Eddy was Boston (although she resided at Concord, 70 miles away).

A master stroke was the establishment in 1908 of the *Christian Science Monitor*, a daily national newspaper. This outstanding paper, winner of dozens of journalistic awards, has given the cult a measure of prestige which other denominations may envy. It avoids sensationalism and abides by certain taboos demanded by the church's philosophy.

Adverse criticism of the cult by others is silenced by the powerful Committee on Publications. Publishers, magazine editors, or bookstores which disseminate material critical of Christian Science are subjected to various forms of boycott and intimidation by the Committee and its local vigilantes. However, its campaign against Dakin's *Mrs. Eddy: The Biography of a Virginal Mind* backfired and turned the book into a best seller in the 1920's. It is now available in a paperback edition.

Christian Science is an urban movement attracting women of the middle and upper classes. Rural churches are scarce and the ladies outnumber the men at least three to one. Church regulations forbid tabulation of membership, but the 1936 census reported 268,915 members. Today, judging from the number of branch churches, we may estimate about 350,000 in the United States and somewhat fewer than 100,000 in England. The cult registered its greatest gains between 1900 and 1926.

The devout Christian Scientist begins her day by reading selections from the writings of Mrs. Eddy. She attends Sunday morning worship services and the Wednesday evening testimonial meetings. Here members describe the supposed healings they have experienced. Following Mrs. Eddy's injunction Scientists usually abstain from liquor, tobacco, and coffee. Children of Scientists attend Sunday school until they become 20. Qualified Scientists, members of the Mother Church, may enroll for a two-week class instruction taught by an approved teacher. Graduates form an elite within the cult. Low women on the totem pole are those who attend a branch church but are not members of the Mother Church.

The church supports no eleemosynary institutions except for a few rest homes. The Principia, a liberal arts college in Illinois, is operated by Christian Scientists but is not owned by the church itself.

Like Jehovah's Witnesses, Christian Scientists find themselves involved in endless legal battles and disputes with authorities. They object to compulsory physical examinations in the schools, vaccination programs, X-rays, fluoridation of water supplies, the teaching of the germ theory of disease in biology, expenditures for medical care out of the public treasury or community chests. Most public institutions bend over backward to accommodate those with religious scruples.

Supposedly everyone may apply the healing principles of Christian Science. Actually a special class of healers, known as practitioners, do most of the systematic healing of difficult cases. The 10,000 practitioners are listed in phone books, keep regular office hours, and charge standard fees for office and house calls. They attempt to persuade the sufferer of the unreality of pain and disease by prayer and reading from the works of Mrs. Eddy.

People today are less willing to turn their backs on medicine than they were 90 years ago. They cannot ignore the successes of miracle drugs, X-ray techniques, the Salk polio vaccine, blood transfusions, improved sanitation, etc. If men can now anticipate a life span twice that of their great grandfathers it can be attributed to modern medicine and science, not to Mrs. Eddy's theories.

As for its religious orientation it is hard to extend the term Christian to Mrs. Eddy's system. Christians must ask Christian Scientists how Jesus could have suffered and died on the cross for the sins of mankind if suffering, death, and sin are all phantoms of the mind.

CHAPTER 10

OLD CATHOLICISM

Old Catholics Balked at Definition of Papal Infallibility in 1870

———— • ————

Dozens of Old Catholic churches, many of them nothing but paper churches or products of fertile imaginations, date to the refusal of a minority of Catholics to accept the definition of papal infallibility made by the First Vatican Council of 1869–1870.

Old Catholics can still be found in Holland, Germany, Switzerland, Austria, and the United States. All together they probably number fewer than 500,000 including the Polish National Catholic Church which contributes 300,000 of this world total. These are self-governing churches united by their acceptance of the Utrecht declaration of 1889.

The roots of Old Catholicism in Germany go further back than 1870. A schismatic "German Catholic Church" came into being about 1845. The founders were two priests, Johannes Ronge and Johann Czerski. Later on, by way of protest against the latitudinarianism of the Ronge-Czerski schismatics, Dr. Pribil of Berlin founded the "Protestant Catholic Church." The 1864 encyclical *Quanta Cura* of Pius IX helped to increase the strong antipapal mentality of many German Catholics. Then in the late 1860's Joseph J. Overbeck, a secular priest and professor of Syriac at Bonn, became a Lutheran. He tried to form a Western Orthodox Church, published many books, and continued his campaign until 1884, when the Holy Synod of Moscow finally rejected the scheme.

Schismatic bodies existed in France from 1801 when the "Petite Eglise" came into being. It consisted of bishops and clergy who refused to recognize the concordat between Pius VII and Napoleon. The last priest of this body died in 1847, but it lingered on for at least half a century.

Msgr. Chatel founded the "Eglise catholique francaise" in 1831. He was consecrated by Bishop Fabre-Pallaprat, who had refused to accept the 1801 concordat. This body survived until the 1890's.

Hyacinthe Loyson's schismatic sect in France, formed about 1879, was only loosely associated with the Old Catholics. It was supported at first by two Scottish Episcopalian bishops. In 1888 Bishop Cleveland Coxe of Western New York took this French schismatic body under his wing, and helped to finance it. After Loyson's resignation in 1893 the Dutch Old Catholic bishops agreed to accept his followers into communion.

The first attempt to form a national church in Italy was made at Verona about 1850. One or two attempts were made before 1882 when Count Enrico di Campello, formerly a Canon of the Vatican Basilica, founded the "Chiesa Cattolica Nazionale d'Italia." Campello was reconciled with the Church before his death in 1903.

What we now know as Old Catholicism began when a handful of German theologians refused to accept the definitions of the Vatican Council regarding the infallibility of the pope as well as his supreme and universal jurisdiction.

Resistance was led by the famous church historian Johann Ignaz Doellinger, who declared: "As a Christian, as a theologian, as a historian, as a citizen, I cannot accept this doctrine." The objectors called a meeting in 1871 to organize the schismatic church. About 300 priests and laymen attended, including some Anglicans, Orthodox, and Protestants. By the end of the year 23 schismatic parishes had been established.

The schismatic archbishop of Utrecht attended the next Old Catholic congress in 1872. The movement was looked on favorably by the governments of Prussia, Baden, and Hesse but opposed by the authorities of Bavaria.

Doellinger, who was 70 at the time of the Vatican Council, respected the excommunication imposed on him by Rome and ceased his priestly functions. However, he presided at the Old

Catholic congresses and guided the sect to a repudiation of the Council of Trent. He opposed the abolition of clerical celibacy and asked that his name be removed from the list of Old Catholic clergy for a few years, but it was later included. He received the last rites from an Old Catholic priest at his death in 1890.

Since no bishops had joined the rebellion, the schismatics, desiring episcopal consecration, turned to the Church of Utrecht. This ancient diocese had gone into schism in 1704 after refusing to endorse Rome's stand against the Jansenist heresy. Later, a missionary bishop, Dominique Marie Varlet, stopped for ten days in Amsterdam on his way to assume the post of bishop of Babylon. He had been in charge of French missions in what was then the Louisiana territory. He received his appointment in 1718 as coadjutor bishop of Babylon and sailed for France. On the day of his consecration in Paris he got word that the bishop of Babylon had died and that he was no longer coadjutor but bishop. He agreed to confirm 600 children in the schismatic church. Bishop Varlet continued his journey by way of Russia to Persia. Here he was informed that he had been suspended for performing episcopal functions for the schismatics and for failing to call on the papal nuncio in Paris to give his adhesion to the Bull *Unigenitus*. He returned to Holland and settled in Amsterdam.

The leaders of the Church of Utrecht finally prevailed upon Varlet to consecrate a bishop for them. He consecrated Cornelius von Steenoven in 1724 and when the latter died Varlet consecrated three other men. Through the last of these, Peter John Meindaerts, consecrated in 1739, all genuine Old Catholic bishops now trace their apostolic succession.

For many years after its break with Rome the Church of Utrecht continued to observe all the canonical formalities. Its leaders notified the pope when they elected a new bishop and informed him of the consecration. The popes regularly replied by issuing bulls of excommunication. At the start of the schism three out of five Catholics in Holland belonged to this national church; by 1815 only 6000 remained in the Church of Utrecht while almost one million were in communion with Rome.

It was to this remnant that the German and Swiss Old Catholics appealed. They knew that these Utrecht orders were undoubtedly valid although considered irregular by Rome. A German Old Catholic priest received episcopal consecration from Utrecht in 1873. A bishop for Switzerland was consecrated in 1876.

In 1899 the various Old Catholic bodies drew up a statement of doctrine called the Declaration of Utrecht. Five Old Catholic bishops adopted this joint statement. Among other things they agreed not to consecrate other Old Catholic bishops without the consent of the other bishops. The Declaration of Utrecht also repudiated the Council of Trent: "We refuse to accept the decrees of the Council of Trent in matters of discipline, and as for the dogmatic decisions of that council we accept them only so far as they are in harmony with the teaching of the Primitive Church." No longer could the Old Catholics maintain that they represented the pre-1870 Roman Catholic Church since that Church had obviously accepted the disciplinary and doctrinal decisions of Trent for hundreds of years.

Some governments favored the Old Catholics as a counterforce to Rome but the politicians soon recognized that this schism was heading nowhere. The Old Catholics supported Bismarck's Kulturkampf and received special legal favors in return.

Most Old Catholic clergy were ex-Roman Catholic priests. Over a period of years the Old Catholics rejected the obligation of auricular confession, fasting, indulgences, the Index, stipends, the doctrine of the Immaculate Conception, veneration of relics, the Latin liturgy. It recognized the validity of Anglican orders in 1925 and has in recent years come under Anglican influence.

The daughter churches of Germany, Switzerland, and Austria moved much faster than Utrecht in disciplinary changes. For example, the Old Catholic Church in Switzerland abolished clerical celibacy in 1875 and the German Church followed suit two years later, but the Dutch Church retained this regulation until 1922. Most Old Catholic bishops are now married as are practically all Old Catholic priests. In Austria the Old Catholics allow divorce and cremation, thus attracting some Roman Catholics looking for an "easier" church home.

Power in the independent Old Catholic churches rests in a synod. Synod membership includes the bishop or bishops, members of the synodal council, all priests of the diocese, and lay representatives of the parishes.

Before World War II the European Old Catholics numbered about 170,000. The instigators of the schism had expected that large numbers of Roman Catholics would join the movement, but their hopes were in vain. The Old Catholic churches lacked dynamic leaders and suffered through alliances with anticlerical governments which sought to use them as a tool against Rome.

During the war Old Catholic churches were destroyed, priests killed, congregations dispersed. The German, Dutch, and Swiss Old Catholic Churches belong to the World Council of Churches. They agreed to send observers to the Second Vatican Council.

At present we estimate about 40,000 Old Catholics in Germany, 40,000 in Austria, 30,000 in Switzerland (where the church is called the Christian Catholic Church), and about 12,000 in Holland. The Communists dissolved the Old Catholic churches in Poland and Czechoslovakia.

The Polish National Catholics obtained their orders from the Dutch Old Catholics in 1907. (See Chapter 15.) The PNCC far outnumbers the rest of the Old Catholics today and it is the only Old Catholic body in the United States in fraternal relationship with the original continental Old Catholics.

For the most part the bodies claiming to be the Old Catholic Church in this country are the shaky creations of religious entrepreneurs. Ordinations and consecrations are often bought and sold. Membership statistics are highly suspect and many congregations exist only in the imaginations of the patriarchs, exarchs, primates, metropolitans, archbishops, and bishops of the tiny sects. They are plagued by feuds and defections.

Some of these Old Catholic sects trace their origin to the remarkable and pathetic adventurer, Joseph Rene Vilatte, born in 1854.

His father was a Parisian butcher, and he was brought up in an orphanage. He emigrated to Canada after the Franco-Prussian War, but returned to France for his military service. On being told that he would have to serve seven years in the army, he fled to Belgium, where he entered a community of the Christian Brothers at Nau Namur.

He left Belgium in 1876, and sailed for Canada, feeling that he was called to the secular priesthood. The bishop of Montreal sent him to the College of Saint-Laurent, where he studied for three years under the Holy Cross Fathers. What happened next is not quite clear. It appears that he fell under the influence of the apostate priest, Father Chiniquy, who had become a Presbyterian minister, and who, in addition to publishing scurrilous books exposing the errors of Romanism, had elaborated his thesis that the Jesuits had assassinated Abraham Lincoln. According to Vilatte's own story he then resumed his studies at McGill University for two years. During this period, he tells us, he was much troubled by religious doubts.

He appears to have been reconciled with the Roman Church at least once, and found hospitality with several religious communities both in Canada and the United States, finally with the Clerics of St. Viator at Bourbonnaise, Illinois. Here he met Pastor Chiniquy again, who advised him to go to Green Bay, Wisconsin, where the Belgian settlers were ripe for conversion to Protestantism. Chiniquy also suggested that Vilatte should write to Loyson, the onetime Carmelite monk, who had formed a sect known as the Gallican Catholic Church.

It was early in 1884 that Vilatte, still a layman, started work as a free-lance Presbyterian missionary in Wisconsin, with the chief object of converting the French and Belgian settlers around Green Bay. About a year later, apparently on the advice of Loyson, he approached J. H. Hobart Brown, Protestant Episcopal bishop of Fond du Lac, suggesting that the Presbyterian mission should be taken under his protection as an Old Catholic outpost.

Bishop Brown agreed to this, and in 1885 arranged that Vilatte be ordained deacon and priest by Bishop Herzog, the Old Catholic bishop in Switzerland. On his return to Wisconsin he worked for three years with great zeal, but after the death of Bishop Brown in 1888, and the appointment of Father Grafton (a "Cowley Father") as his successor, the situation became difficult. Vilatte wanted to be raised to the episcopate.

At first Bishop Grafton was prepared to consider this, but it did not take him long to realize that Vilatte was an ecclesiastical promoter, who behind his back was negotiating at the same time with the Roman Catholic bishop of Green Bay, the Russian Orthodox bishop of the Aleutian Islands, and the Old Catholic bishops in Europe. In 1890 Vilatte severed all relations with the Episcopal Church, and on May 29, 1892, managed to get himself consecrated by Julius Alvarez. Alvarez was formerly a priest of the Latin rite, who had formed a schismatic sect known as the "Independent Catholic Church of Goa and Ceylon," after he had been raised to the episcopate in 1889 by Mar Paul Athanasius, Syrian Antiochene bishop of Kottayam. Vilatte was given the title of "Mar Timotheas, Archbishop of the Old Catholic Church of America." It was alleged that his consecration was performed with the permission of Ignatius Peter III, Jacobite patriarch of Antioch.

Once he got back to Wisconsin, Vilatte realized that he had not gained much by his journey to Ceylon. The bishop of Green Bay secured the services of French- and Flemish-speaking Premonstratensian canons to counteract further conversions to Old Catholicism. At no time did Vilatte have a large following around Green Bay.

By 1894 he was in touch with Archbishop Satolli, the first Apostolic Delegate to the United States, and with the Bishop of Green Bay, seeking reconciliation with Rome. Nothing came of these negotiations, and Vilatte, realizing that the game was up, turned his attention to the Poles, who were having difficulties with the American Catholic bishops. In 1898 he consecrated Stanislaus Kaminski at Buffalo. Then he returned to Europe where in the course of the next two or three years he was responsible for forming small schismatic bodies in England, France, and Italy by ordaining priests and consecrating several bishops.

Early in 1899 it was announced that Vilatte was in Rome and about to make his submission to the Pope, but in the end he left

Europe and found a refuge in Canada for some years, hard up financially and pursued by his creditors. He was back again in France in 1906 where he laid the foundations of the schismatic Eglise Francaise Catholique. For the next few years he made Chicago his headquarters, and in 1915 founded there what he called the American Catholic Church. He retired from the primacy in 1920. The following year he consecrated the first bishop for the African Orthodox Church, after which he returned to his native France. In 1925 he made his formal recantation of errors, and it is said that it was the Pope who asked the Cistercians of the Abbey of Pont-Colbert, near Versailles, to give him a home.

He was not allowed to celebrate Mass, and grew restless. Shortly before his death in 1929 he ordained secretly one of the novices, and even raised him to the episcopate! He was buried as a layman, although a number of Catholic theologians were prepared to admit that his orders were valid. Cardinal Merry del Val, however, maintained that throughout his episcopal career Vilatte had so "commercialized" ordinations and consecrations, that he himself was not able to regard them as valid. In fact, it is difficult to believe that this adventurer was ever sincere in anything he undertook — even his final "conversion."

Vilatte's schismatic sect in the United States, known as the American Catholic Church, is reported to have 5000 members in 29 churches — probably a generous estimate. Even this tiny group has split into two factions. It is amply served by an archbishop, two auxiliary bishops, and a titular bishop.

James Francis Augustine Lashley, who started the American Catholic Church, Archdiocese of New York, at the latest report in 1947, claimed 8000 adherents in 20 churches, all in New York City.

Perhaps the largest surviving sect launched by Vilatte is the African Orthodox Church. The Rev. George Alexander McGuire withdrew from the Episcopal Church in 1919 to found a separated Negro Episcopalian church. He first called his churches Independent Episcopal churches but changed the name to African Orthodox in 1921 and received consecration as bishop from Vilatte. Some of the members of the African Orthodox Church, under the leadership of

Reuben Spata, a native of Uganda, are now in full communion with the Orthodox patriarch of Alexandria. They have adopted the Byzantine rite.

The African Orthodox liturgy is a combination of the Anglican, Roman, and Orthodox liturgies. It recognizes seven sacraments. McGuire now claims the title of patriarch and the African Orthodox Church reports 24 churches and 6000 members. One of McGuire's bishops broke off and formed his own African Orthodox Church of New York in Harlem.

In 1914 Prince de Landas Berghes et de Rache, who had been consecrated by A. H. Mathews the previous year, was forced to flee to the United States as an enemy alien. On his own authority he consecrated two men as his suffragans. His purpose was to unite the Old Catholic factions, but he only added to the confusion. De Landas was reconciled with the Holy See before his death in 1920.

One of his suffragans, William Henry Brothers, set up the Old Catholic Church in America and in turn consecrated about half a dozen bishops. The other suffragan, an ex-Catholic priest by the name of Carmel Henry Carfora, organized the North American Old Roman Catholic Church. He consecrated more than 20 bishops not only for his own body but for various national groups.

Carfora who gave himself the title "Supreme Primate" and claimed infallibility when he spoke ex *cathedra* died in Chicago in 1958. At his death his church claimed 78,000 members in 60 parishes. Since his death this body has split into four or five factions. One is headed by Carfora's former chancellor, Primate Metropolitan Hubert A. Rogers of Brooklyn, and another by a former bishop of the Carfora church, Richard A. Marchenna, who was suspended at least twice by Carfora.

The remnant of the Brothers' sect, reduced to himself and two or three priests, was received into union with the Patriarchal Exarchate of the Russian Orthodox Catholic Church in America in 1962. All were reordained and Brothers is now a Mitred Archpriest.

Both the Rogers and Marchenna factions claim substantial memberships which they duly report to the editor of the *Yearbook of American Churches*. The editor is in no position to verify such statistics so that since Carfora's death the number of quasi-Old Catholics appears to have risen dramatically. As a matter of fact the number has probably declined.

The tiny Reformed Catholic Church (Utrecht Confession) maintains its headquarters in Los Angeles. Its estimate of membership is modest: 2217 in 20 parishes. It claims to be part of a worldwide Reformed Catholic Church with congregations in England, France, and Germany. Its archbishop, W. W. Flynn, states, "We have no arguments with Rome — she is our mother and we respect her as such." The Flynn group criticizes Utrecht for falling under Anglican domination.

Another minuscule body is the Western Orthodox Communion of the Old Catholic Church headed by the Right Reverend Sir Mar Michael Augustine Itkin, KT, of New York City. Itkin also belongs to the American Humanist Association, which rejects the idea of God, immortality, and the supernatural. He is assisted by three other bishops. The Yearbook for 1962 gives its membership as 2570.

The bizarre Liberal Catholic Church also derives its orders from Mathew, consecrated Regionary Old Catholic Bishop for England in 1908, but its theosophical and occult orientation puts it beyond the pale of orthodox Christianity. (See Chapter 16.)

At the time of writing, the principal organizations in America claiming the Vilatte succession are the following. The names in parentheses indicate the present head of each body: African Orthodox Church (W. E. J. Robertson); African Universal Church (E. J. Anderson); American Catholic Church, Syro-Antiochean (E. L. Peterson); American Holy Orthodox Catholic Apostolic Eastern Church (C. C. J. Sherwood). In Europe there are about half a dozen sects also claiming the Vilatte succession.

Among the bodies claiming the Mathew succession represented in North and Central America are: Independent Episcopal Church (W. P. Crossman); Liberal Catholic Church (A. G. Vreede); Liberal Catholic Church, American Schism I (E. M. Matthews); Christian Catholic Church (H. S. Spruit); Mexican Old Roman Catholic Church (J. P. Ortiz); North American Old Roman

Catholic Church (R. A. Marchenna); Old Catholic Church in North America (G. T. Billett); Old Roman Catholic Church in North America (H. A. Rogers).

In addition to the above there are the following organizations, most of them claiming lines of succession from Latin or Eastern sources: American Catholic Church, Archdiocese of New York (F. Lashley); Apostolic Polish Church of Canada (P. A. R. Markiewicz); Byzantine American Church (A. J. Aneed); Eastern Orthodox Catholic Church in America (J. M. Moreno); Holy Orthodox Church in America, Eastern Catholic and Apostolic (T. De Witow); Mariavite Church of Poland (?); North American Orthodox Church (A. T. Turner); and the Reformed Catholic Church, Utrecht Confession (W. W. Flynn).

It appears that, so far as doctrine is concerned, many of these bodies are tainted with theosophy and other heresies. Few of them can be regarded as either "Catholic" or "Orthodox." Lastly, it is difficult if not impossible to check up on them, because of the tendency to split up into subschisms. Although many of them claim to be Old Catholic, none is recognized by the genuine Old Catholic Churches of Holland, Germany, and Switzerland. Few are in communion with any other schismatic bodies; they lead an independent existence. None is recognized by the World Council of Churches, except the Polish National Catholic Church.

Since 1931 the Old Catholics of Europe have been in intercommunion with the Anglicans. The PNCC likewise entered into an agreement of intercommunion with the Protestant Episcopalians in 1945.

The genuine continental Old Catholics claim to stand for Catholicism undiluted by the errors of Rome. They accept the seven sacraments, the ancient creeds, and a number of Catholic practices. Some of their clergy have drifted into the seas of rationalism and Protestantism since the original 1871 break.

Last year at the International Congress of Old Catholics in Haarlem, The Netherlands, the delegates adopted a statement declaring their readiness to enter into a full fellowship with the Eastern Orthodox. Copies were sent to the heads of the various

Orthodox churches. The Congress received goodwill messages from the Orthodox patriarchs of Moscow and Istanbul.

In many ways the quasi-Old Catholic bishops in the United States resemble the *episcopi vagantes* of the early Church — bishops without jurisdiction or recognized authority. A student of this movement placed the number of such men with possibly valid episcopal orders in this country at 120.

The Catholic Church follows the Augustinian theory that a bishop who is validly consecrated retains the power to transmit valid but irregular orders. In practice, the Church ignores orders received by apostates from schismatic bishops. These men, if reconciled to the Church, need not recite the divine office or even observe celibacy.

Rent by schisms and feuds, the so-called Old Catholic bodies in the United States present a confusing picture. In some cases they consist of a primate, an archbishop, and several bishops, and one store-front cathedral.

CHAPTER 11

JEHOVAH'S WITNESSES

Watchtower Society Warns Mankind
Against Impending Battle of Armageddon

———— • ————

Had Catholics of the world multiplied as fast as the ranks of Jehovah's Witnesses in the past twenty years, we would find no more than a handful of non-Catholics left. From 71,000 Witnesses in 1939, to more than 920,000 today, the aggressive, Brooklyn-based cult has earned the title of the world's fastest growing religion.

Most of this spectacular growth has been reported since the death, in 1942, of the cantankerous and aloof "Judge" J. F. Rutherford. His successor, Nathan Knorr, the Watchtower's business manager, inaugurated a face-lifting and public relations program which is paying dividends in converts.

Most of us probably remember the old-style Jehovah's Witness who called at our homes, often on a Sunday morning. He wasted few words telling us he was giving us a rare opportunity to survive the coming battle of Armageddon.

A smile or kind word was enough to set him to winding his portable phonograph to play a four-minute sermonette by "Judge" Rutherford. With slight encouragement he would try to sell a copy of the *Watchtower* magazine or the latest scripture-heavy book by the Judge. A show of disinterest or the explanation that you and your family were quite satisfied with your Catholic religion would release a torrent of abuse and dark hints about your eternal destiny.

No longer do the door-to-door evangelists tote a portable phonograph and a collection of Rutherford's records. A thorough training in speech, apologetics, and salesmanship enables the experienced Witness to deliver his own Bible talks.

The infuriating, one-foot-in-the-door approach has been abandoned. An indication of disinterest by the householder no longer touches off a torrent of abuse and threats of Jehovah's vengeance. Today's "new look" Witness smiles, pets the dog, speaks softly, and accepts rebuttals and door slams with some degree of graciousness. Don't worry. He or a fellow Witness will be around your neighborhood again next year.

Anyone who shows interest in the cult's message of impending doom for this old, wicked world will be urged to buy a magazine or a copy of *Let God Be True*, a 320-page exposition of their curious theology. It sells for fifty cents. More than ten million copies were printed for the first edition in 1946, and since then almost seventeen million have been distributed.

Each Witness tries to devote at least sixty hours a month to proselytizing, selling *Watchtower* or *Awake!* on street corners, or studying the Bible. Many "publishers," devoting only enough hours to secular employment to support themselves, spend every spare minute warning others of the imminent battle of Armageddon. An elite class of full-time Pioneers directs the work of local congregations and seems to be fulfilling the role of the clergy in the sect.

The molders of Witness strategy know how to manipulate mankind's natural feelings and fears. Who has not thought of the destructive force of A-bombs and H-bombs, ballistic missiles, overpopulation scares, corruption in high office, TV-quiz riggings, influence peddling, the spread of pornography, and natural disasters without at least a fleeting temptation to despair? The problems of the world seem so complex and the evil so pervasive that many souls are ready to throw up their hands in discouragement and resignation.

This is precisely what Jehovah's Witnesses have done. They have resigned from the world. Its problems, wars, and politics no longer concern them; they claim to be citizens of a far better society, Jehovah's New World theocracy.

Witness writers and speakers tell us over and over that the old world is dead and the New World has taken its place. Before long, Christ Jesus will lead the forces of Jehovah against Satan and his worldly cohorts in the battle of Armageddon. When the dust of this greatest battle in history finally settles, the wicked will have disappeared into nothingness along with death, sickness, and evil.

They believe all worldly governments — democratic, Communistic, Fascistic — usurp the power of Jehovah's theocracy and have become, one and all, simply tools of Satan. The Witnesses refuse to serve these governments. Their self-imposed neutrality explains why Witnesses refuse to enter the armed forces, salute the flag, vote, or hold political office.

Failing to understand this basic position, some people think the Witnesses are pacifists like the Quakers and Mennonites. On the contrary, the Witnesses worship a vengeful God who plans the bloodiest war in history: Armageddon. They would gladly take up arms for Jehovah in the forthcoming struggle and seem to savor realistic descriptions of the fate of the wicked who are slain for allying with Satan's armies. Witnesses hold no scruples against shedding blood in such a war but refuse to become involved in the petty squabbles of Satan's nations.

For legal reasons, during World War II they claimed exemption from the draft on the basis that all Jehovah's Witnesses are ordained ministers of the gospel. Most courts disagreed and denied deferments to part-time Witness-preachers who held regular jobs. More than 4000 Witnesses were sentenced to penitentiary terms for disregarding draft-board induction notices. Canada and Australia banned all Witness activities during the war.

To trace the development of Witness theology, we must go back to 1872 when a 20-year-old Pittsburgh haberdasher, Charles Taze Russell, wandered into an Adventist meeting and discovered the doctrine of the imminent Second Coming. To this doctrine Russell coupled a denial of the existence of hell. To explain the frequent biblical references to hell, Russell declared that *sheol* should be interpreted to mean the grave. Man is not immortal nor does he possess a soul. When he dies he enters a sort of "soul sleep" rather than heaven, hell, or purgatory. What Adam lost for mankind at the Fall was life everlasting, said Russell.

He began teaching small Bible classes around the Pittsburgh area and soon broke with Adventism. He called a meeting of the Protestant ministers in the vicinity and presented his novel interpretations of Scripture, and he seemed genuinely surprised when they remained unconvinced. This angered the new prophet, and he turned against all religion, Protestant and Catholic, as a racket and a snare.

As his movement gained momentum, Russell toured the nation and Europe, founded the original *Watchtower* magazine and legal corporations, and devised a photo-drama of creation which employed lantern slides and records. "Pastor" Russell pinpointed the Second Coming in 1914 and for more than forty years prepared his flock for the event.

To his dismay, 1914 came and went. Most of the pastor's followers, however, persevered through the shabby divorce actions by Mrs. Russell and showed no concern when the pastor juggled his property holdings among his several corporations to avoid alimony payments. A hard core swallowed his $60-a-bushel Miracle Wheat, his phony cancer cure, and his wonderful Millenniel Bean. With such loyalty, they would not desert him just because he miscalled the Second Coming.

Pastor Russell recalculated the dates of his prophecy and took a second look at some proof texts. He discovered that the Second Coming had actually taken place in 1914 but that, contrary to everyone's expectation, it was an invisible event. Christ and Satan had battled in the heavens, and now Christ was enthroned. Satan was thrown out of heaven and was forced to do his mischief in the vicinity of earth. This, he declared, explains World War I and all the troubles which have beset the planet since then. Soon after announcing this news, Russell passed away on a Pullman car while returning from a preaching tour of California.

The Watchtower's legal adviser, J. F. Rutherford, took over the operations in 1917. A small-town, Missouri lawyer, Rutherford had taken his turn as acting judge in the absence of the elected judge and thereafter appropriated the title in recognition of his four days on the bench. Admittedly, with wing collar, string tie, and cane, he looked more like a judge than most judges.

Rutherford set out to consolidate his position as president of the society by outfoxing the majority of the board of directors in a neat legal maneuver. He jettisoned some of Russell's pet theories, such as the Great Pyramid system whereby the pastor claimed to be able to foretell history by measuring the rooms of the Egyptian pyramids. Russell's books were discontinued, and the Judge's own voluminous, scripture-laden writings began to roll off the cult's printing presses.

His career as president of the Watchtower Society was soon interrupted by a prison term at Atlanta penitentiary. He and six other officials were sentenced to 20-year terms on a charge of sedition. After the armistice they were released and the federal government eventually dropped its case. Meanwhile the organization had practically suspended activities.

Once Rutherford assumed control again he intensified publishing and missionary efforts. He introduced the portable phonograph technique which enabled tongue-tied Witnesses to bring the Judge's voice into millions of homes.

For 25 years the Judge turned out books and pamphlets, brooded, and avoided the personal appearances in pulpit and platform that his predecessor enjoyed. He sprinkled relevant and irrelevant Bible passages on every page of his luridly illustrated tracts. In 1931 he announced a new name for the cult: Jehovah's Witnesses. Before this they were known as Millenniel Dawnists, Russellites, International Bible Students, Watchtower people, and the like.

To broadcast its message of impending doom for this old world the society purchased a radio station on Staten Island and offered to furnish recorded lectures by Rutherford to other stations. Eventually the anti-Catholic character of these talks alienated sympathetic station owners who feared adverse reaction by Catholic listeners and advertisers.

Rutherford's orneriness infected converts to the cult. Stanley High would write in 1941 that the cultists knew no peers for "conscientious cussedness on a grand scale." Malcontents, disgruntled Catholics, paranoiacs, and oddballs enlisted in Rutherford's New World Society.

Though he coined the watchword "Millions Now Living Will Never Die," the Judge himself died in 1942. He spent the last years of his life in a mansion near San Diego, California, which the cult had purchased for occupancy by Noah, Abraham, Abel, and other prophets and princes who were expected to return to earth before Armageddon.

Knorr turned the society into an anonymous, efficient machine. No books or magazine articles nowadays give any indication of authorship although presumably Knorr himself contributes many manuscripts. Correspondence from Brooklyn is not signed but merely stamped "Watch Tower Bible and Tract Society." Rutherford's books have gone the way of Russell's. Only two remain in print.

Jehovah's Witnesses are fundamentalist unitarians. They constantly ridicule the doctrine of the Trinity and flatly deny the divinity of Christ. References in Scripture to the Holy Spirit are taken to mean merely the power of Jehovah.

They believe that Jehovah God (their favorite title for the deity), created a spirit-son Christ Jesus, who, before becoming man, was also known as Michael the Archangel. This spirit-son, not God but more like a favorite angel, took on human flesh as a perfect man and died as a ransom for mankind, which had fallen in Adam and incurred the penalty of death.

After his death on a torture stake (not a cross, the Witnesses insist), Christ was raised to a new spirit existence by Jehovah. Together with 144,000 selected men who have merited heaven, Christ Jesus will govern the earth from his heavenly throne as a sort of executive director under Jehovah.

His invisible Second Coming in 1914 also heralded the great battle between good and evil. Scripture tells the Witnesses that this battle will positively begin during the lifetime of those living in 1914. Most Witnesses expect Armageddon between 1970 and 1979.

For many decades, the Witnesses concentrated on finding the remaining living members of the 144,000 remnant who will govern the new world from heaven. In 1925, Rutherford instructed them to enlarge their efforts to gather as many as possible of the "other sheep." These latter are thought to be men of goodwill who will join the New World Society and thereby survive Armageddon unscathed.

According to their eschatology, the Witnesses will not actually fight at Armageddon but will observe the battlefield at a safe distance. They will see the wicked and the religionists annihilated. Satan will be bound for a thousand years, and the millions now living who will never die (Jehovah's Witnesses) will begin to repopulate a paradise on earth.

Over the years, the righteous dead will be raised and given an opportunity to declare themselves for Jehovah. Unlike Armageddon's survivors, they will not be allowed to marry and beget children. The wicked stay in the graves, since they have earned no second chance. At the end of the millennium, Satan will be set free to tempt a few away from Jehovah; they and the seducer will finally be annihilated.

Inhabitants of this earthly paradise will live forever. They will enjoy the prime of life, and tend gardens, sing hymns, and play with the now friendly beasts of the jungle. For many people in the "out" group of a society which bestows its choicest rewards on those with more education, social status, wealth, and ambition, this picture of an eternal Garden of Eden and a final comeuppance for those now on top has its appeal.

In Brooklyn, the cult operates Bethel House, where 700 Witnesses live a semimonastic life. Administrators, writers, linotypists, secretaries, and printing pressmen live and work according to a strict schedule. They get room, board, and $14 a month allowance, which is the same for Knorr as for the greenest receptionist.

Their huge presses turn out 4,200,000 copies of the *Watchtower* twice a month in fifty languages. The companion magazine, *Awake!*, goes to 3,750,000 readers. These circulations, together with other signs, such as attendance at the Memorial Service, indicate the existence of a large body of perhaps several million "fellow travelers" in addition to the 920,000 full-fledged Witnesses.

Witnesses are touchy about studies which show that the majority of the cultists come from the economically depressed classes. As a matter of fact, this was probably more true 20 years ago than today.

Nevertheless, surveys show that only one Witness out of 100 holds a college degree. One large, midwestern university enrolls only one Witness in a student body of 14,000.

Many converts undoubtedly find a purpose in life through the cult. They are guided through an adult-education program which gives them enough confidence to discuss the Bible and theology in the homes of perfect strangers. They convince themselves that they have been singled out by Jehovah to survive Armageddon. They boast of their tidiness, their legal victories, their converts, and the circulations of their magazines and books. To date, however, only two persons of any prominence have joined: President Eisenhower's mother and mystery writer Mickey Spillane.

Democratic, congregational government was replaced by theocratic (Brooklyn-directed) control in 1938. A class of Pioneers exercises growing authority over local groups and individual members. Advanced training is now offered at Gilead School in South Lansing, New York, and at Brooklyn headquarters.

Until Armageddon the Witnesses consider themselves aliens in all worldly nations. Since no nation recognizes Jehovah's New World theocracy, all are governments of Satan. Jehovah's Witnesses will have no truck with these false governments. They will not serve in their armies or help fight their wars, vote in their elections, salute their flags, or accept their political offices.

Casual observers of the religious scene sometimes fail to understand the extent of the cult's estrangement from society and its effect on individual members. For example, this "neutrality" is the basic reason why Witnesses object to army service. As citizens of an invisible theocracy they simply claim the rights accorded any aliens. So far, however, they have not refused to pay taxes to support Satan's government and armies and have been conspicuous in appealing to Satan's courts for justice.

Legal fights in this country have centered around their draft status and their refusal to allow blood transfusions and to salute the American flag. The Witnesses have won 36 of the 50 cases to reach the Supreme Court.

During World War II their activities antagonized both the Axis and the Allies. Witnesses found themselves in Nazi concentration camps as well as federal penitentiaries. When a nation is fighting for its life, it is inclined to deal rather harshly with those who refuse to fight, vote, salute the flag, cooperate in community projects, accept political responsibility, buy bonds, donate blood, and the like.

What does the future hold for the cult? For one thing, we know that few Witnesses are born; practically all Witnesses today are recent converts. Experience shows that converts are likely to display a zeal and enthusiasm which birthright members lack. Will second- and third-generation Witnesses generate the same enthusiasm?

The postponement of Armageddon may shake the movement, but a student of religion knows many examples of the resiliency of cults in the face of similar crises. The Witness in 1989 may be telling his neighbors about the invisible Armageddon of 1979.

We can expect the growth of Jehovah's Witnesses to continue for at least another 20 years. Already they number 900,000 members — all of whom are active preachers — and several million fellow travelers. They may possibly become a major force in American religious life in the next decades.

CHAPTER 12

SALVATION ARMY

Salvationists Wage War on
Slumdom, Rumdom, and Bumdom

————— • —————

Few of the millions of Christmas shoppers who will toss a dime or a quarter into a Salvation Army kettle during the holiday season know much about that Army. Is the Salvation Army a welfare agency? a church? a sort of Protestant religious order?

If he has given this any thought, the average American may see the Salvation Army as a vaguely Protestant-related social-welfare organization with an affinity for military methods. As a matter of fact, the Salvation Army is a distinct Protestant denomination with its own creed, clergy, ritual, and seminaries. It serves a lower-class constituency just as the Protestant Episcopal Church generally serves an upper-class constituency.

The Army itself holds no illusions about its primary purpose. In its booklet, *Pilgrim's Progress: 20th Century*, published by the Army's National Research Bureau, we read: "He [the local Army director] conducts a religious, social and recreational program in his Corps building comparable to that of a progressive church" (p. 12). On the next page, the author continues: "These services include first of all, the vital and basic parish work of the Corps officers in the local setting. This is at the very core of all Salvation Army life, since it is the fundamental purpose for which the organization was founded — the salvation of men."

In its war on slumdom, bumdom, and rumdom the Army never forgets that its primary objective is to save souls and to bring the message of the gospel in its evangelical formulation to the poor and troubled.

William Booth (1829–1912) founded the Salvation Army. Baptized an Anglican, he preferred the warmth of the Methodists and became a lay preacher at the age of 17. He once remarked, "I want my religion like my tea — hot." He sought ordination from the Methodist New Connection. His converts, however, were seldom welcomed in regular Methodist chapels and he began to offer church services for the slum dwellers of East London. He first called his work the East London Revival Society and later the Christian Mission, but in 1878 he adopted the name Salvation Army and established the quasi-military form which distinguishes it from the scores of other Protestant churches and sects. The Rev. Mr. Booth became General Booth. Wesley found his converts rejected by the Anglican churches of his time and was forced to set up his own society; Booth found his converts unwelcome at the Methodist churches and followed a similar course.

The change to a military organization not only involved the use of military terminology, ranks, and uniforms, but meant that the government of the Army would be purely and simply autocratic. Officers obey superior officers.

Queen Victoria disliked the idea of an English army not under her control. She objected to Booth's assumption of the title "General." Later English monarchs applauded the work of the Army.

The Army advanced. From the British Isles it crossed the Atlantic in 1880 and found root in Philadelphia and New York. With quick success the General sent expeditions to Australia, France, Switzerland, Sweden, India, Canada, South Africa, Iceland, and Germany.

Only six years after the Army invaded the United States, President Cleveland received a delegation from the Army at the White House and gave the Army his official endorsement. General Booth himself made four inspection trips to America.

It has been said that the American people rediscovered the Salvation Army during World War I. Although the Army had met emergencies in the Spanish-American War and the San Francisco earthquake, it remained for its officers in the trenches of France and its lassies in the canteens to bring its work to the attention of the nation.

In recognition of the Army's war efforts, President Wilson conferred the Distinguished Service Medal on Commander Evangeline Booth, the General's daughter and head of the United States branch. Veterans remembered the Army with affection after the war and helped launch fund drives to build Army citadels (churches) throughout the country.

Just before the war, General Booth had died at the age of 84, blind and penniless. Konrad Algermissen comments: "Although many millions of dollars had passed through his hands, he died a poor man. With him there died a man of which it can justly be asserted that within the Catholic Church which, alas, he hardly knew, he would have become a second Francis of Assisi" (*Christian Denominations*, p. 856). The General's wife Catherine had died of cancer in 1890 after bearing eight children and helping her husband in the works of mercy. Algermissen writes: "With the sacrificial spirit of a St. Elizabeth of Hungary, she had devoted herself to the salvation of the poorest of the poor" (p. 855).

Today the Salvation Army operates 1279 churches in the United States with a membership of 250,156 and another 160,678 children in its Sunday schools. Its extensive programs are supervised by 3851 ordained officers who are assisted by part-time local officers and soldiers (members).

Throughout the world the Army operates 367 hostels, 66 employment bureaus, 39 general hospitals, 37 maternity hospitals, 90 maternity homes for unwed mothers, 141 children's homes, 27 hotels. It publishes 137 periodicals. Staffing these institutions are 27,000 officers and cadets in 86 countries.

Contrary to popular misconception the Salvation Army does not recruit many of its officers from ex-boozers or reformed bums. Those whom the Army helps and/or converts are reestablished in the community and may retain membership in the Army as soldiers. This membership corresponds to membership in the Methodist or Baptist Church. They may purchase and wear an Army uniform and devote spare hours to evangelistic work. The Army, however, usually looks to other sources for its officers.

Rarely do college graduates seek careers as Salvation Army officers and the Army sets no such educational requirement. "Vigor of mind, consecration to and enthusiasm for the service and other qualities of character and personality" are valued above college degrees. Most candidates nowadays have finished high school and many come from Salvation Army families, i.e., families in which the parents serve as full-time officers.

A young man or woman who wishes to become an officer usually begins as a corps cadet under the instruction of a local officer. During this six-month probationary period the suitability of the candidate may be judged and he or she may get some idea of the type of life which officership involves and the sacrifices it demands.

After this probationary period, he may make a formal application. If he gets the nod from the candidate board he enters one of the four training centers at New York, Chicago, San Francisco, or Atlanta. Here the buck private pursues a two-year course in Bible, sociology, social work, physiology, domestic science, public speaking, English, music, accounting, and Army rules and regulations. The school arranges field trips to courts, hospitals, skid rows, welfare agencies, etc. The Army displays slight interest in art, philosophy, or literature unless these are directly related to evangelism.

As might be expected, the training school follows a military routine. A bugle wakes students at 6:30 a.m. and sounds lights out at 10 p.m. Each private takes care of his own bed and handles chores around the buildings and grounds. There are no servants.

Following graduation as probationary lieutenants or captains, the new officers take additional correspondence courses and read a book a month on Salvation Army history or activities. When they pass examinations on these subjects they become fully commissioned officers.

Each officer gets furnished quarters and a salary ranging from $28 a week for an unmarried officer just commissioned to $45 for a married couple. Extra allowances are given for children, experience, reasons of health.

Length of service and efficiency determine promotion. From captain the officer may advance to adjutant, major, brigadier, lieutenant colonel, colonel, lieutenant commissioner, and commissioner.

A wife takes the rank of her husband. An officer who marries a civilian retains the title "Reverend" but must leave the Army. Marriage outside the Army is strongly discouraged.

Salvation Army brides are expected to wear their uniforms to the altar instead of the traditional white bridal gowns. An Army manual also suggests that Salvation Army tunes would be more appropriate at the ceremony than wedding marches. The couple enters the marriage not only for love for each other "but because we believe that the union will enable us better to please and serve God and more earnestly and successfully to fight and work in the Salvation Army."

Divorce is forbidden except for adultery. In a divorce both officers must resign from the Army but the innocent party may apply for readmission after a few years. It is almost always granted.

Salvation Army officers may conduct worship services, perform marriages, bury the dead. They qualify as clergymen in every way and may serve as chaplains in the armed forces. As we have seen, however, they receive a minimum of formal educational and theological training.

Women have played a prominent role in Salvation Army history. Evangeline Booth headed the Army in the United States for over 30 years and directed the worldwide organization for five years. Women hold equal rights with men in all phases of Army life and the Salvation Army was among the first Protestant denominations to ordain women. Today there are more women officers than men in the United States and all officers are ordained ministers.

A general at International Headquarters in London gives the final word on all matters of management, doctrine, and discipline. He appoints all higher officers. A commissioner directs the Army branch in each country around the world.

At the death of a general the commissioners and territorial commanders assemble in London to elect a successor. The present general is Wilfred Kitching who grew up in a Salvation Army family himself.

Basic evangelistic techniques include the familiar street meeting. Each corps is expected to sponsor its own brass band. Once a crowd gathers, the band leads the way to the citadel, where the prayer meeting features gospel hymns, Bible reading, preaching, and testimonials. In a recent year, the Army counted 25,000 converts in the United States, of whom about a third enlisted as soldiers.

In recent decades the Army has extended its program beyond the slums and skid rows. It now conducts youth programs, day and summer camps, homes for unmarried mothers, day nurseries, hospitals, prison rehabilitation, a missing-persons bureau, servicemen's canteens, disaster relief, an antisuicide bureau. Most centers collect used clothing, old newspapers, and repairable furniture. The paper is sold to mills for reprocessing, while the clothing and furniture are repaired and resold at nominal prices to low-income families.

Military terminology pervades the Army to an extent that an outsider finds rather amusing. What another church would call a creed the Army calls its "Articles of War." Converts become recruits and soldiers. Prayer meetings are known as "knee drills." Officers get "furloughs," not vacations; they get "marching orders" to new assignments. Eventually they are "promoted to glory" and a bugle blows taps over their graves. They wear a military uniform, progress through a system of ranks based on that of the British Army, receive a salute.

Two schisms do not seem to have hampered the growth and reputation of the Army.

Major Thomas E. Moore, head of the United States territory, refused to obey General Booth's order to take command of the work in South Africa. Instead he founded a rival Salvation Army in 1884 and took the title of general. His group was known as the Salvation Army of America while the parent body was known as the "Worldwide" or English Salvation Army. Eventually the international Army prevailed and most of the American Salvationists were reconciled to it in 1889. A few posts refused to return to English rule and reorganized in 1913 under the name the American Rescue Workers. Their theology is similar to that of the Army, but they observe baptism and the Lord's Supper. The Workers operate 35 churches with 2350 members. They work mainly in the East with headquarters in Philadelphia,

The general's son, Commander Ballington Booth, left the Army in 1896 to found the rival Volunteers of America. He objected to the autocratic and foreign control of the Army and wished to introduce more democracy in its government. The Volunteers also restored the sacraments. They have done their most notable work among prisoners and parolees. Ballington served as general of the Volunteers of America until his death in 1940. His wife succeeded him until her own death in 1948 and her place was taken by a son, Charles Brandon Booth. Last year the Volunteers of America counted 28,230 members in 204 churches.

Understandably, the Salvation Army prefers not to advertise the fact that it constitutes a separate and distinct church. Its acceptance by some United Funds and Community Chests might be jeopardized if it emphasized its religious objectives. Algermissen explains: "The Salvation Army wishes to be super-denominational. But since it possesses a separate religious doctrinal system, separate religious customs, a separate religious organization, it must be reckoned among the others as a Christian sect" (p. 859).

Fr. John A. Hardon, S.J., passes the same judgment: "In reality the Army is a Protestant sect in the fullest sense of the term, with a mandatory body of doctrine, following a prescribed ritual and worship, and governed by a well defined ecclesiastical authority" (*The Protestant Churches of America*, p. 277).

The Army itself quotes the decision of the Judge Advocate General of the United States in 1917 after a study of the question to determine if Army officers could qualify as chaplains:

It seems that the Salvation Army is a world-wide religious organization, with followers in great numbers, property in generous measure, and doing great good. It has distinct legal existence; a recognized creed and form of worship; a definite and distinct ecclesiastical government; a formal code of doctrine and discipline; a distinct religious history; a membership not associated with any other church or denomination; a complete organization, with officers ministering to their congregations, ordained by a system of selection after completing prescribed courses of study.

In common with other churches, it has a literature of its own; established places of religious worship; regular congregations;

regular religious services; a Sunday-school for the religious instruction of the young, and schools for the preparation of its ministers. The functions of its ministers seem to be similar to those of the clergy of any other church. In addition to conducting religious services upon stated occasions, they perform marriage ceremonies, bury the dead, christen (dedicate) children, console the bereaved and advise and instruct the members of their congregations.

Catholics should have no interest in attempting to exclude the Salvation Army from community-wide fund raising, since much of the Army's work is an exemplification of the corporal works of mercy rather than a religious indoctrination. So long as other social agencies such as the St. Vincent de Paul Society do not become labeled as "sectarian" in contrast to the supposedly "nonsectarian" Salvation Army or YMCA, there seems to be no reason why the generosity of the public should not assist these Christians in feeding and housing and clothing the poor.

On the other hand, we can imagine no circumstances which would allow a Catholic to serve on the local board of the Salvation Army, to contribute directly and substantially to the building fund for a local citadel (church), to subscribe to the *War Cry* magazine, to direct others to evangelistic meetings.

Fr. Francis J. Connell, C.SS.R. states: "The Salvation Army is a Protestant movement, in which many sincere and good Protestants participate. But it is not a movement in which Catholics may actively participate." Father Connell sees no harm in contributing to food baskets: "But to co-operate toward the spread of the organization in itself, which includes the propagation of non-Catholic doctrines, is entirely forbidden to those who believe that Jesus Christ established only one religion, and that the religion which He established is promulgated only by the Catholic Church" (*American Ecclesiastical Review*, February, 1956, p. 24).

No organization of comparable size has done more to help the friendless, the poor, the down-and-outers than the Salvation Army. To some the Army means a meal and a flop for the night, to others a doughnut on a distant battlefront, to still others a home where a mother without a wedding band may bring her baby into the world.

The dedicated Salvation Army officers quietly and patiently carry out the words of our Lord that "Whatever you have done to these, the least of My brethren, you have done to Me."

CHAPTER 13

UNITY SCHOOL OF CHRISTIANITY

*Unity Offers Gnostic Christianity
Mixed With Oriental Religions*

———————— • ————————

Not many people imagine that Catholicism and Christian Science are compatible. An informed Catholic who would regularly consult a Christian Science practitioner would be a rare bird.

But many Catholic families subscribe to the attractive magazines published by a quasi-Christian Science cult: the Unity School of Christianity of Lee's Summit, Mo. The cult's six main periodicals reach more than 1,000,000 homes each month. They include *Daily Word*, *Good Business* ("a magazine that teaches business people to think in terms of success"), *Unity*, *Weekly Unity* (for novices), *Wee Wisdom* for young folks, and *Progress* for teen-agers.

Charles W. Ferguson has called Unity "An enormous mail-order concern dispensing health and happiness on the large scale of a modern business enterprise. It is mass production in religion and its work is carried on shrewdly and systematically."

Headquarters of this religion-by-mail is a 1200-acre "campus" at Lee's Summit, a village about 18 miles from Kansas City. Here are located its printing plant with 12 rotary presses, administration building, 165-foot tower of Silent Unity, tennis courts, golf course, swimming pool, stocked 22-acre lake. More than 700 men and women, almost all devotees, work at Lee's Summit.

Heart of the Unity movement is the work of Silent Unity. Each year more than 600,000 appeals for prayers and healings pour into this department. They come by telephone, letter, and telegram. A corps of 100 Unity adepts work around the clock to pray for the intentions received and to answer letters. Unity makes no charge for its services in the spiritual realm but accepts love offerings which furnish most of its annual budget.

Unlike Christian Science, to which it is closely related, Unity does not demand that its followers sever membership in their former churches nor does it disparage the faith of those who continue to accept medical care. What Unity furnishes is a gnostic "higher interpretation" of Christianity. It claims it is not a church or sect but only a "nonsectarian religious educational institution." We are forced to doubt this statement.

Unity trains its own ministers at Lee's Summit and ordains those who complete specified requirements. Through its field service it maintains contacts with 200 Unity Centers in the United States which function like local churches. The Unity ritual provides for a baptism ceremony (with rose petals for infants), communion, marriage, funeral, and installation of officers. Unity worship services are similar to the typical Protestant service and consist of hymns, prayers, and a sermon; the Wednesday evening meeting features healing testimonials.

Charles Braden, author of several books on American cults writes: "It [Unity] has actually developed into a sect which does have its own local membership, its own meeting places, its own worship services, and its own ministers. Indeed, it is indistinguishable in most respects from any other religious denomination" (*These Also Believe*, p. 146). The largest number of Unity Centers are in California, Florida, Illinois, Michigan, Missouri, New York, Ohio, and Washington.

Founders of Unity were a bankrupt real-estate broker and his wife, Charles and Myrtle Fillmore. Charles, who had the advantage of only a few years of schooling, worked successively as a printer's devil, a bank and grocery clerk, a bookkeeper in a railroad freight office, mule-team driver, assayer, and real-estate broker. He made and lost a fortune in the Kansas City real-estate boom in the mid-1880's.

Fillmore suffered from a hip disease, curvature of the spine, and deafness, and his wife, a former schoolteacher from a Methodist background, was a TB victim. Both were plagued by ill health and sought relief in various healing systems. Finally Myrtle Fillmore claimed to have discovered the secret of spiritual healing. Her watchword was "I am a child of God and therefore I do not inherit sickness." She converted her husband to her ideas.

Both the Fillmores had been students of Christian Science but had never agreed completely with Mrs. Eddy. The official historian of the movement states: "From the first issue of his magazine *Modern Thought*, we know that Charles Fillmore also had a knowledge of such teachings as Buddhism, Brahmanism, Theosophy, and Rosicrucianism, as well as of Christianity" (James Dillet Freeman, *The Story of Unity*, p. 40). Fillmore once wrote one of his followers that he and his wife had enrolled in more than 40 courses in metaphysical and occult subjects, some costing as much as $100. The eclecticism of their theology is obvious.

On one occasion Fillmore entertained a Catholic visitor at Lee's Summit and accompanied her to Sunday Mass. Freeman relates that he "astonished his friend by explaining to her the symbolical meaning of every part of the ritual of the Mass" (p. 41). It is possible that his explanations might also have surprised a liturgist.

In the beginning the couple called their magazine *Christian Science Thought* but Mrs. Eddy objected to the usurpation of the name and the Fillmores eventually changed it to *Unity*. The pair devoted themselves entirely to the cult after 1889.

Over the years they expanded their publications, set up a successful vegetarian restaurant in Kansas City, established a broadcasting station in 1920, taught classes in their healing methods. They had become the American publishers of Swami Vivekananda, who introduced Yoga to these shores. Mrs. Fillmore thought up the idea of Silent Unity which has been one of the most popular attractions of the cult.

To identify Unity publications they adopted the symbol of a winged globe. It appears on all periodicals and letterheads. Fillmore explained: "It is an ancient Egyptian symbol and I remember that when I first saw it I felt that I had had something to do with it in a previous incarnation."

The system the Fillmores constructed was a blend of Christian Science and New Thought, Theosophy, Hinduism, Vegetarianism, Christianity, Yoga, and assorted other philosophies. The Unity idea of God is pantheistic, impersonal: "God is not a being or person having life, intelligence, love, power. God is that invisible, intangible, but very real, something we call life" (H. Emilie Cady, *Lessons in Truth*, p. 18). Like Christian Science, Unity uses traditional Christian terminology to express radically different meanings.

Myrtle Fillmore died in 1931. Charles later married his secretary and bought a home in the San Fernando Valley in which he spent his winters. He died in 1948 at the age of 94. His two sons, Lowell, 80, and Rickert, 78, continue to direct the activities of the Unity school.

Claims of membership in Unity depend on the definition used. Some estimates run as high as 5,000,000 and no doubt this many people have read or been influenced by Unity publications and ideas. Those who regularly attend Unity Centers and give their total allegiance to Unity probably can be numbered at a few hundred thousand. Many people read Unity magazines and contact Silent Unity for help but have no thought of leaving their own Methodist, Baptist, Presbyterian — or Catholic — Churches.

The cult disguises its own teachings in some of its popular magazines such as *Wee Wisdom*, oldest children's magazine in the country. Freeman explains: "*Wee Wisdom* has always presented the Unity idea and expressed a positive Christian philosophy of life, but it has kept its material so free from 'preaching' that the majority of parents, teachers, and children do not even class it as a religious publication" (p. 73–74). He adds, "The connection of Unity with it has always been kept in the background" (p. 75).

Unity healers, unlike Christian Science practitioners, do not charge for their services. Both weekly and monthly magazines sell for only $2 a year. Nevertheless, the cult has acquired property valued in the millions of dollars and pays union wages to printers, binders, secretaries, and other help.

One successful fund-raising scheme has been the Prosperity Bank. Unity mails out thousands of these cardboard banks with instructions for their use. Adherents meditate on the "Prosperity Prayer" whenever they drop a coin in the bank. After seven weeks they are told to mail the bank to Lee's Summit.

Unity believes that it is God's will that man be strong, vigorous, rich, successful, and happy. Fillmore said, "Some religious teachers have tried to make us believe that it is our Christian duty to be poor. But this is not the doctrine of Jesus." Fillmore's metaphysical interpretation of the twenty-third Psalm appears in his book *Prosperity* as follows:

> The Lord is my banker; my credit is good. He maketh me to lie down in the consciousness of omnipotent abundance; He giveth me the key to His strong-box. He restoreth my faith in his riches. He guideth me in the paths of prosperity for His name's sake. Yea, though I walk through the very shadow of debt I shall fear no evil, for Thou art with me; Thy silver and gold, they secure me. Thou preparest a way for me in the presence of the collector; Thou fillest my wallet with plenty; my measure runneth over. Surely, goodness and plenty will follow me all the days of my life; and I shall do business in the name of the Lord forever.

What does Unity teach? The movement reverences the Bible but seeks inspiration from other scriptures as well, such as the Upanishads and the Koran. It is relativistic regarding religious truth: "The differences in religions seem to be due primarily to the different interpretations put upon spiritual truths by the leaders of each (world religion), and to forms of worship, which unfortunately often tend to obscure the beauty and simplicity of the original principles" (Turner, *What Unity Teaches*, p. 4).

Unity claims to represent primitive and practical Christianity. Freeman maintains: "Unity is the Truth that is taught in all religions, simplified and systematized so that anyone can understand and apply it" (p. 61).

Unity students are taught to repeat certain denials and affirmations. The four chief denials are as follows:

> There is no evil.
> There is no absence of life, substance, or intelligence anywhere.
> Pain, sickness, poverty, old age, and death cannot master me, for they are not real.

There is nothing in all the universe for me to fear, for greater is He that is within me than he that is in the world.

The affirmations include one that reads: "I am Spirit, perfect, holy, harmonious. Nothing can hurt me or make me sick or afraid, for Spirit is God, and God cannot be sick or hurt or afraid." Students are taught to abandon their old ideas of a personal God, a devil, sin, original sin, heaven and hell. Fillmore wrote in the January, 1936, issue of *Unity*: "Stick to it . . . and say 'I am not a sinner. I never did sin. I cannot sin. I am from above.'"

Jesus was a man who developed His divine nature, known in Unity terminology as the Christ, to the fullest. "The difference between Him and us is not one of inherent spiritual capacity but a difference in demonstration" (Turner, p. 8).

Charles Fillmore did not accept the inevitability of death and often affirmed that he could escape the reaper. Both he and his wife believed in and taught reincarnation and embodied this doctrine in the teachings of Unity. The cult's statement of faith declares: "We believe that the dissolution of spirit, soul and body caused by death, is annulled by rebirth of the same spirit and soul in another body here on earth. We believe the repeated incarnations of man to be a merciful provision of our loving Father to the end that all may have the opportunity to attain immortality through regeneration, as did Jesus." Charles even claimed to know who he had been in previous incarnations.

Most Unity students are vegetarians, but the cult does not insist on this. After a special revelation to Charles Fillmore they added fish to the menu of their vegetarian restaurant. Unity forbids the use of alcohol and tobacco and limits the use of sex to procreation.

The cult employs the most modern methods of communication. Its giant presses turn out more than 2,000,000 printed pieces each month including magazines, books, and tracts in many languages. Five magazines are printed in Braille and distributed free to the blind.

Unity sold its radio station but furnishes recorded programs to 50 cooperating stations in the United States, Australia, and New

Zealand. Its devotees keep pamphlet racks stocked in railroad depots and other waiting rooms.

Incidentally, Unity resembles in many respects Norman Vincent Peale's brand of Christianity. Marcus Bach of the State University of Iowa has observed: "Every contemporary writer in the field of positive thinking, peace of mind and peace of soul is in debt to this school."

In order to accept the religious orientation of the Unity School of Christianity a Christian would have to abandon belief in the resurrection of the body in favor of the doctrine of reincarnation as well as belief in the basic Christian doctrines including the Trinity.

CHAPTER 14

PENTECOSTALISM

Pentecostals or "Holy Rollers"
Seek Gifts of First Pentecost

———— • ————

"In the name of Jesus Christ I command you, Satan, to leave this man's body and free him from his sickness," screams the perspiring preacher as he shakes a young man of about 18. Voices in the tent repeat "Praise Jesus" and "Amen." The young man stares straight ahead, smiles weakly, whispers something to the preacher, and shuffles along to the side of the platform. A long line of the afflicted winds its way to the platform.

These dozens of people have come to the healing revival, confident that Jesus will cure them through the special power of the faith healer. The revival may last a week. For as long as two hours before the healing part of the service the audience has sung gospel hymns, prayed, contributed love offerings, heard the rapid-fire preaching of several revivalists. After the exorcism they will probably leave the tent with the same afflictions with which they came.

Millions of Americans belong to churches which feature faith healing. To them the Christian message consists primarily in maintaining or recapturing physical health. Disease is the effect of sin, probably personal sin. Faith in Christ will drive the demons of sickness from their bodies.

Of the hundreds of practicing faith healers who pastor churches, conduct healing revivals around the country, and broadcast on radio and TV stations none has attained the popularity of a 44-year-old Pentecostal preacher from Tulsa, Oral Roberts. His organization is the General Motors of the faith-healing world.

Since 1947 Roberts has conducted revivals in most of the major United States cities and several foreign countries. His films depicting his healing "successes" are shown on 129 TV stations and his weekly sermons are carried on 332 radio stations. The Oral Roberts Evangelistic Association in Tulsa employs 415 people, including those who man the "Secret Place" which offers 24-hour-a-day intercession for those of the faithful who write in and contribute love offerings.

The main seven-story headquarters building includes a 1500-seat auditorium, editorial offices, mail rooms, staff offices. Here the directors of the bustling Association plan the 11 major campaigns held each year. Few brain surgeons command a larger income than the Rev. Roberts.

According to Roberts' own testimony he was miraculously cured of stammering and TB at the age of 17. He was the son of a farmer-preacher and his wife of Pontotoc County, Oklahoma. Following his own healing experience he became an itinerant minister himself. He spent time on and off in two small denominational colleges but failed to win a degree. Roberts married his guitar-playing wife in 1938 after borrowing $18 to pay for the ring and license.

He became pastor of the tiny Pentecostal Holiness Church in Toccoa, Georgia. Oral Roberts was convinced he had received a special healing power from God but he failed to heal many clients or win many adherents. Finally he began a long fast which resulted in a loss of 32 pounds. At the conclusion of his fast he decided to risk everything and rent an auditorium in Enid, Oklahoma. He claimed to achieve a number of spectacular healings at these meetings and his career was finally off the ground.

In Tulsa he packed a large tent every night for nine weeks. Rumors that he had actually cured a blind man spread throughout the area and people came on crutches and in wheelchairs to hear the dynamic young preacher and see if he could bring them back their health.

Since then Oral Roberts' team has carried on healing revivals in most American cities as well as in Japan, Poland, Finland, Puerto Rico, and Canada. He ran into trouble in Australia. A group of

Protestant ministers denounced him and a weekly newspaper called him "at best a big blabbermouth." The crowds in Australia were small: seldom more than 5000 in a tent which seated 14,000.

Groundwork for the Roberts' entourage is usually handled by local Pentecostal and Holiness churches which sponsor his crusades. The Pentecostals believe that the powers of apostolic times were lost by an apostate church but can be received by fervent Christians. These powers include not only faith healing but "speaking in tongues." At the height of an emotion-packed prayer meeting someone in the congregation may begin to utter strange sounds which are believed to be foreign or ancient languages. Sometimes another member of the congregation will try to interpret the message.

Actually we distinguish two branches of this Holiness movement. One branch, known as the Perfectionists, includes the Church of the Nazarene, the Church of God (Anderson, Indiana), the Pilgrim Holiness Church, and the Christian and Missionary Alliance. These Perfectionists believe that man can attain perfection through a baptism of the Holy Spirit. They preach the original Wesleyan doctrine of entire sanctification which has been quietly dropped by the larger Methodist Church. They also practice faith healing.

The more radical or left-wing branch of the Holiness churches is the Pentecostal. The Pentecostals insist that speaking in tongues, glossolalia, is a necessary part of this baptism of the Holy Spirit. Largest of the Pentecostal churches is the 500,000-member Assemblies of God, but this radical branch includes numerous store-front cults and backwoods snake-handling groups.

The baptism of the Holy Spirit is an instantaneous transformation following justification. It frees the Christian from all depravity wrought by original sin. The Christian who receives this second blessing can also exercise the gifts of Pentecost such as healing the sick.

They also emphasize foreign mission work and in several South American countries the Pentecostals far outnumber converts to the more traditional Protestant churches. There, as in the United States, they generally attract people of limited education, wealth, and social standing.

Do Oral Roberts and the other faith healers heal? We would never say that certain people who come to his revivals do not leave free from an affliction which may have plagued them for years. To explain these healings as miracles of God's power, however, is something else. The hypnotist and psychiatrist also heal, but we do not call their powers supernatural.

If people are freed of afflictions, the answer probably lies in the area of mass suggestion, psychosomatic medicine, and hypnotism. We know relatively little about these forces, but they are being brought forward to explain many healing phenomena.

In the healing revival the illnesses themselves are usually self-diagnosed. If a believer says he is suffering from chest pains, arthritis, deafness, cancer, a tumor, or whatever — the healer and the audience take him at his word. If he later testifies that he has been miraculously healed, he is also believed. No doctors are called upon to verify the malady or the cure. No one follows up the "healings" to see if they are permanent or if the healed are anything but neurotics or publicity seekers or confederates.

That certain physical ailments are tied up with complex mental mechanisms is clear. Some physicians estimate that 90 percent of the people in their waiting rooms are suffering from mental-related afflictions. So far the Rev. Oral Roberts has produced no cures which a qualified board of physicians and psychiatrists would declare inexplicable by natural means.

Msgr. John E. Kelly explains: "Oral Roberts' films are carefully edited versions of his tent services with only the more plausible cures presented to viewers. Those whom God does not heal on the spot by the touch of Roberts' right wrist, who say they still can't see or hear, are brusquely dismissed with the clergyman's rebuke that if they haven't been healed it's only because their faith is weak."

One of the most pathetic scenes I have ever witnessed was at a healing revival in my hometown. Two children had brought their mother to the service. She was gray and bent and must have been in her 80's. When her turn came to approach the visiting healer, one of her daughters explained that the mother was deaf and sought to recover her hearing. The healer prayed, screamed, and shook the old lady but obviously she remained almost stone-deaf. Finally, he explained to the children that their mother lacked faith in Jesus and was still possessed by the devil. The mother wanted to know what had been said and the faith healer shouted into her ear that she was still possessed by the devil. The woman began to cry and her children led her off the platform. The flushed healer motioned for the next patient to step forward.

Oral Roberts lives well. He flies to meetings in the Association's own plane, usually stays at the city's leading hotel. He has said: "Christ has no objection to prosperity." His income, estimated at over $150,000 a year, comes from the love offerings taken up at the conclusion of the healing campaigns and from royalties on his books. He, his wife, and four children live on a five-acre estate near Tulsa. He has recently sold his prize herd of Angus steers which had been the object of some criticism.

Collections at a successful healing revival may reach several thousand dollars a night. Devotees may sign up for the "Blessing Pact" and agree to send $10 to $25 and more each month to the Tulsa office to promote the work. At a New York City luncheon last year 40 supporters signed pledges for $600 each to finance a series of foreign-language films about Roberts' ministry.

Several million people belong to the various Perfectionist and Pentecostal churches. While the Assemblies of God claims more than 500,000 adult members in the United States, it enrolls more than 1,000,000 people in its Sunday schools. It was organized at a convention in Hot Springs, Arkansas, in 1914, and now reports congregations in every state of the union and 72 foreign countries. In the United States it is strongest in the South and Middle West.

Active in missionary efforts, this denomination ranks first in the number of overseas Bible schools and fifth in the total number of foreign missionaries. Its home missions are directed toward the Spanish-speaking, Jews, Indians, prisoners, the deaf, and the blind. Its aggressive missionary spirit has resulted in the formation of almost one new church a day in recent years.

International headquarters are maintained in Springfield, Missouri, where 500 employees handle church affairs and operate a huge printing plant which turns out five tons of literature a day.

Another colorful Pentecostal body is the creation of Aimee Semple McPherson: the International Church of the Foursquare Gospel. The thrice-married lady evangelist built a 5300-seat auditorium in Los Angeles where she used every theatrical device to win attention. She disappeared mysteriously in 1926 and turned up later with an account that she had been kidnapped and tortured but had escaped from a desert hideout. When she died in 1944 her son Rolf assumed leadership of the Foursquare Church which now reports 83,000 adherents. This sect supports 400 missionaries, most of whom are in Latin America.

Another large Pentecostal body is the Pentecostal Holiness Church, of which Roberts is an ordained minister; it claims 105,000 members. The Church of God (Cleveland, Tennessee), one of many sects using the name Church of God, claims 170,000 members and 270,000 Sunday school pupils.

In the Perfectionist wing of the Holiness movement, the Church of the Nazarene is the largest. Formal organization of this body was undertaken at Pilot Point, Texas, in 1908. Most of the founders were former Methodists who wanted greater emphasis on Holiness doctrines. Sociologists see the Church of the Nazarene as a textbook example of a sect changing to church status. This group is gradually assuming the characteristics of the older, more established denominations. It dropped the word "Pentecostal" from its title in 1919 and now seems to be dropping "Holiness" from its colleges and publications.

Most Perfectionist and Pentecostal churches share a Puritan outlook on entertainment, liquor, tobacco, the Sabbath, gambling. Their members are likely to tithe their incomes to support the church and its missions. The average per capita contribution may exceed $100 a year (this is per member not per family).

Pentecostalism adopts the doctrine of justification by faith alone of the Lutherans, the attitude toward baptism of the Baptists, the church government of the Congregationalists, the entire sanctification beliefs of the early Methodists, the missionary methods of the

Salvation Army. To these Pentecostalism adds its own doctrines of speaking in tongues and faith healing.

The Holy Rollers may be a source of amusement to those in the older and more respectable denominations but they can also teach others a few lessons in missionary zeal, church support, mass evangelism, and the value of Sunday School promotion. Their emotionalism, lack of social consciousness, and anti-intellectualism will probably never appeal to the middle or upper classes, but they will continue to win converts from the poor and uneducated — of whom there are hundreds of millions on this planet.

CHAPTER 15

POLISH NATIONAL CATHOLICISM

*Nationalism Precipitated Only Major
Schism in American Catholicism*

———— • ————

During its history the Church in the United States has suffered only one serious schism. Today that schismatic body, the Polish National Catholic Church, claims to enroll more than 282,000 members in this country in addition to constituents in Poland and Canada. This would mean that about one of 20 of the more than 5,500,000 Americans of Polish ancestry gives allegiance to the PNCC.

With 157 parishes the PNCC labors among Polish Americans concentrated in the nine states of Massachusetts, Connecticut, New York, New Jersey, Pennsylvania, Ohio, Michigan, Illinois, and Wisconsin. It is served by four bishops and 144 priests in the United States who claim valid orders through the Old Catholics and the Church of Utrecht.

Externally its church buildings resemble Catholic churches built half a century ago. PNCC churches include altars and tabernacles, sanctuary lamps, stations of the cross, numerous highly colored statues, crucifixes, confessionals, holy-water fonts, etc. The average visitor might imagine he was attending a Roman Mass except for the difference in liturgical language: Polish instead of Latin. These outward similarities, however, disguise a radical doctrinal departure as we shall see.

The Poles were not converted to Christianity until A.D. 1000. Protestant ideas spread by the Hussites and Lutherans were squelched by the Jesuits of the Counter Reformation and by 1600 the Reformation effort in Poland was dead.

During the latter part of the nineteenth century thousands of Poles entered the United States. The trickle became a flood and in the peak year of 1912–1913 more than 175,000 Poles passed through Ellis Island. These immigrants tended to settle in ethnic and language communities, mostly in the nine states mentioned. The Christian Poles were practically all Roman Catholics and have remained devoted to the Church; today there are hardly more than 5000 Polish Protestants in the country.

These newcomers discovered that the Church of their fathers was not directed by fellow Poles in America but by bishops of Irish and German descent. Even though these bishops helped establish the more than 850 predominantly Polish parishes and parochial schools, a few ultranationalistic Poles objected to non-Polish direction. They seemed to yearn for some sort of separate but equal policy such as the various Eastern rites enjoy.

A lack of Polish priests sometimes made it necessary to appoint non-Polish pastors over Polish parishes. A few congregations here and there rebelled and sought to win the right to choose their own pastors. They refused to listen to preaching in English and were reluctant to follow the established forms of property control set up by the Council of Baltimore.

The PNCC developed in this setting from three separate independence movements originating between 1895 and 1900. Fr. Antoni Koslowski, who had been assistant pastor of St. Jadwiga Church in Chicago, organized an independent congregation of All Saints in 1895. He obtained consecration as a bishop by the Old Catholics in Switzerland in 1897, and in the next ten years started 23 schismatic parishes from New Jersey to Manitoba. He called his creation the Polish Old Catholic Church. Koslowski died in 1907 without having consecrated any bishops.

A second stream of dissent which ended in the PNCC began when Polish parishioners in St. Adalbert Parish in Buffalo objected to the bishop's control of church property. They organized a rival parish called Our Lady of the Rosary in 1895.

Their pastor, Fr. Stanislaus Kaminski, paid $2,500 to Joseph Rene Vilatte, the ecclesiastical adventurer, to be consecrated a bishop.

(See Chapter 10 for Villate's story.) Bishop Kaminski remained a one-parish bishop until his death in 1911. At that time his successor, an excommunicated Roman Catholic priest, got the property transformed to the Catholic bishop of Buffalo, but the courts returned the church to the schismatics in 1915.

The mainstream of the present PNCC started in Scranton in a parish of miners and factory workers. These immigrants had built a church called the Sacred Heart of Jesus but, like the Poles in Buffalo, they did not want to turn over the title to the bishop. For this stand and other actions they were reprimanded by the bishop. Eventually the dispute led to a free-for-all fight in front of the church and the arrest of 20 people.

The disgruntled parishioners appealed for help to a former Scranton curate now in nearby Nanticoke, Father Francis Hodur. The Polish-born Hodur declared: "Let all those who are dissatisfied and feel wronged in this affair set about organizing and building a new church, which shall remain in possession of the people themselves. After that, we shall decide what further steps are necessary."

They followed his advice, raised funds for a new building, and asked the bishop to bless it. He agreed provided they would transfer the title to him in accordance with the Baltimore decrees. They refused.

Father Hodur now became their pastor and named the new church St. Stanislaus. He went to Rome in 1898 to seek concessions for the Polish dissidents, saw two cardinals, but got no satisfaction. He canceled an audience with the Holy Father and sailed for home. Father Hodur was excommunicated on October 22, 1898, and publicly burned the notice of excommunication before the congregation.

The first Mass in the Polish language was celebrated on Christmas eve in 1900. Other Poles began to form independent congregations that were gathered into a synod which met in 1904. By this time the movement had attracted about 16,000 adherents. Hodur was elected bishop but would have to wait three years for consecration.

The European Old Catholics were unwilling to consecrate a second Polish bishop since they had already consecrated Koslowski.

When the latter died, however, they agreed to consecrate Hodur. This was done in St. Gertrude Church in Utrecht.

Hodur managed to incorporate most of Koslowski's parishes into his new PNCC as well as the large Buffalo church headed by Kaminski. To provide insurance benefits forfeited by their apostasy the Polish Nationals set up the Polish National Union in America which has been a financial success. Refused burial in Catholic cemeteries, they bought ground for cemeteries of their own.

Bishop Hodur encouraged a small group of Lithuanians to organize a parallel Lithuanian National Catholic Church in 1914, which persists to this day with four small churches.

At the PNCC's fourth synod in 1921 the church officially authorized the new mission in Poland. Four more bishops were elected and would subsequently be consecrated by Hodur alone. This synod also approved the marriage of the clergy, but few priests took advantage of the ruling because of lay opposition. Today an estimated three out of four PNCC priests are married but newly ordained priests must agree to remain single for two years. Any parish council may refuse to accept a married priest as pastor. Hodur himself never married.

Bishop Hodur got around to consecrating the four new bishops in 1924 in Scranton. One was assigned to the eastern diocese, one to the western, one to Poland, and one to the Lithuanians. When this last died no successor was appointed; the LNCC is now visited by PNCC bishops.

From 1926 to 1936 the sect grew from 61,874 members to 186,000. Hodur had himself trained a few priests to supplement the former Roman priests who formed the original clergy. He bought a three-story building on a busy Scranton corner where he established his seminary called Savonarola after the 15th century Dominican who was hanged as a heretic in Florence.

The seminary now enrolls between 12 and 16 students. Its three-year course is practical: Bible, church history, Polish history, moral and doctrinal theology, philosophy. Students need no college preparation nor do they need to study Latin, Greek, or Hebrew. Courses are taught in Polish, which has become something of a problem since few young men know the language well enough for classroom instruction.

The warden is a former Roman Catholic priest from Poland, Theophilus A. Czarkowski, who is assisted by a few PNCC priests in the area. Men are ordained on Trinity Sunday as deacons and then priests. A fourth year of training is optional. The sect also has a second seminary in Cracow.

Hodur headed the PNCC for almost 60 years. Blind and paralyzed for his last eight years, he used a microphone to deliver sermons from his rectory to his Scranton cathedral. He died February 16, 1953, at the age of 86. Three Episcopalian bishops took part in his funeral rites.

Dominating the life of the Polish Nationals for so many decades, the freethinking Bishop Hodur stamped his own peculiar theological notions into its fabric. What began as a protest against essentially disciplinary measures such as the form of property control, the language of the liturgy, and the power to choose pastors, turned into the muddy waters of doctrinal innovation. Closer relations with the Episcopalians and Old Catholics may enable the present PNCC leaders to reconsider some of Hodur's theological bequests.

A sympathetic historian of the schism, the Rev. Theodore Andrews of the Protestant Episcopal Church, observes: "They [the creedal statements] are, of course, clearly intended as watchwords for a small but venturesome group; and their limitation is that of their being chiefly the work of one author, whose writings are not so much the carefully considered statements of a theologian as homilies of a crusading priest, eager to stir his people to action, and indignant at the pretensions of an alien hierarchy" (*The Polish National Catholic Church in American and Poland*, pp. 39–40).

Hodur's free thought might be illustrated by his statement: "The leaders of the PNCC are of the opinion that before God and before America all beliefs, all sects, are equal. If God did not wish a certain sect to exist, He would not give it the necessary powers to exist and develop."

The PNCC accepts the first four ecumenical councils and its own general synods as authoritative. Some questions on which Hodur spoke, such as the doctrine of original sin and eternal punishment, seem to be considered open questions today which may be defined in some future synod.

That Hodur himself denied the doctrines of original sin and hell is clear. He also maintained that faith is "helpful to man toward his salvation, though not absolutely necessary" (*U. S. Census of Religious Bodies*, 1936).

One of the bishop's theological inventions was the elevation of the preaching, reading, and hearing of the Word of God to the status of "a great sacrament of a Christian, National Church." To end up with seven sacraments he combined baptism and confirmation into one sacrament.

As for the doctrine of the church, the PNCC declares in its current catechism: "All baptized people who are united with Christ through faith are members of the Holy Catholic Church" (p. 37). In answering the question of the need for national churches, the catechism states: "Christ called all men from all nations and races to serve God, each to contribute its particular spiritual and cultural gifts toward the building of God's Kingdom on earth" (p. 40).

Private confession is required of children and young people up to the age of 21. After that the general confession is sufficient. The Polish Nationals still distribute communion under the species of bread only. Communicants must make either a private or a general confession and fast from midnight.

They have made some minor changes in the Roman liturgy but still celebrate the Mass, hold Benediction, have Stations of the Cross, recite the rosary. They continue the special Polish devotions to the Sacred Heart and the Lenten "Gorzkie Zale." The liturgical language is Polish although the pressure is now on from younger members to adopt more English. A few parishes use English in preaching at one or more Sunday Masses.

Hodur added a number of unique feast days to the PNCC calendar; the feasts of the Poor Shepherd, the Polish National Catholic Church, the Remembrance of the Dear Polish Fatherland, Brotherly Love, and the Christian Family. The church holds special liturgical commemorations for Polish heroes and religious reformers such as Huss, Savonarola, and Peter Waldo.

The catechism recommends that all PNCC homes have a crucifix, holy water, and blessed candles. It also sanctions such sacramentals as the sign of the cross, the Angelus, holy oils, ashes, palms, incense, and images of our Lord and the saints (p. 34).

Both parishes and dioceses are relatively autonomous. Authority in the areas of faith, morals, and discipline resides in the clergy; in social and economic matters in the laity.

Every four years the bishops, pastors, and lay delegates meet in the General Synod. Delegates are chosen on the original basis of one for every 50 parishioners — which is becoming rather unwieldly. The four United States dioceses are the Central (Scranton), Eastern (New England), Buffalo-Pittsburgh, and Chicago.

Bishop Hodur's coadjutor did not become Prime Bishop but ended up as pastor of a small parish in Manitoba, Canada. Instead, the bishop of the Chicago diocese, Leon Grochowski, succeeded to the post of Prime Bishop. As a student at Warsaw Polytechnic College, Grochowski participated in forbidden underground activities against the Russians and had to flee to the United States. He was ordained in 1910 by Hodur and was one of the four bishops consecrated in 1924. He was an energetic organizer for the PNCC in the Chicago area and has made 11 trips to his native land. Bishop Grochowski is now 75 and married.

The Prime Bishop, who also heads the Central diocese, consecrates other bishops, controls the seminary and church publications, and examines candidates for the priesthood. The bishops are elected by the synod from a list of eligible priests submitted by the Prime Bishop.

The PNCC discourages formation of religious orders. It operates only one parochial school, a bilingual school in Scranton. The rest of the religious instruction is carried on through classes on Saturdays and Sundays in each parish. The church owns its own printing plant and a 400-acre farm at Waymart, Pa., used as a summer camp and as a home for the aged.

Hodur sent a bishop to Poland in 1925 to take charge of the

mission to the homeland. He also consecrated Wladislaw M. Faron as bishop in 1930 but soon learned that Bishop Faron was beginning to remarry divorced people and had himself consecrated two suffragans without authority from Scranton. Hodur deposed Faron in 1931 and the latter rejoined the Roman Catholic Church in 1949.

The founder of the PNCC visited Poland 14 times. He finally consecrated another bishop for the Polish mission, Joseph Padewski, in 1936. By 1939, the PNCC in Poland claimed 56 parishes, a seminary, and about 50,000 faithful. Few priests in Poland dared to marry. A number of priests lost their lives during the war so that by the end of the war only 70 PNCC priests survived.

The Communist government seemed to favor the growth of the schismatic church as a counterforce to the Vatican, but in 1951 the Reds decided to shut off all contact between the PNCC in Poland and the parent body in the United States. Bishop Padewski was imprisoned and died in a Red prison in Warsaw on May 10, 1951.

With the bishop out of the way the Reds installed their own nominees on the church council. Recently the Gomulka government has imposed a 65 percent tax on the income of the Roman Catholic Church and other "private associations" which is retroactive for ten years. At the same time, the government defined the PNCC as a "public association" and therefore exempt from this tax. The PNCC probably enrolls about 60,000 people today, a tiny fraction of the Polish population. The government's hot-and-cold attitude toward the schismatics is reminiscent of the attitude of Bismarck toward the Old Catholics of his day.

Isolated by a self-imposed language barrier and ultranationalistic aims, the PNCC has only recently entered into the wider fellowship of Protestant and Orthodox bodies. Holding membership in both the National Council of Churches (since 1957) and the World Council of Churches (since 1948), the PNCC has also observed intercommunion with the Protestant Episcopal Church since 1946.

The statement governing this intercommunion points out: "Intercommunion does not require from either Communion the acceptance of all doctrinal opinion, sacramental devotion, or liturgical practice characteristic of the other, but implies that each believes the other to hold all the essentials of the Christian faith." The agreement was based on the Bonn agreement with the Old Catholics on the continent in 1931.

Recently the PNCC has been cooperating with the Puerto Rican National Catholic Church headed by Fr. Hector Gonzalez. Bishop Grochowski confirmed 272 members of this schismatic body in 1961.

Since 1946 more than 70 Episcopal bishops have been consecrated and, of these, approximately half claim succession through both the Anglican and PNCC-Old Catholic successions. Rome has never officially reported on the validity of these PNCC orders. Nor has the role of coconsecrator ever been spelled out. The PNCC bishops served as coconsecrators.

Some Catholic theologians believe that the PNCC orders would be valid since they derive from the generally recognized valid orders of Utrecht. Others doubt whether the Polish Nationals can still claim valid orders on the basis of defect of intention. Konrad Algermissen states: "The validity of episcopal consecration in the Church of Utrecht cannot be doubted, nor in this regard can that of the Old Catholic Church, which depends upon the former" (*Christian Denominations*, p. 349).

Senior Priest Walter Slowakiewicz granted the author an interview in the rectory of Holy Name of Jesus PNCC in Milwaukee. (Since then he has become dean of the mother church of the denomination in Scranton.) Father Slowakiewicz served as pastor of the only PNCC in the city, although two other parishes in the suburbs care for other Polish Nationals in the Milwaukee area. His own parish counts 225 families and 89 individuals for a total of 897 souls. Only a dozen or so families still live within walking distance of the church; the rest are scattered through the city and travel several miles to attend Sunday Mass.

The pastor himself was baptized in the Roman Catholic Church and made his First Holy Communion as a student in a parochial school. His parents took him out of the Catholic Church when they helped establish a PNCC in his hometown.

Father Slowakiewicz married in his 40's; he and his wife have no children. He has no close contact with Catholic priests although his parish is situated in the middle of Milwaukee's heavily Catholic South Side. Relations with Episcopalian and Orthodox clergy are cordial.

He showed me through his church, which is kept locked during the day to protect it from vandals. He says a daily 8 a.m. Mass and three Masses on Sunday. The church interior was recently redecorated but retains the flavor of the 1910's in its many statutes and banners.

The PNCC does not allow divorce and remarriage, although the Prime Bishop may grant annulments. It has made no statement for or against contraception. Father Slowakiewicz said that his church does not forbid membership in any society not condemned by the state, which means that the Polish Nationals may join the Masonic lodge and other secret societies.

A sect based on extreme nationalism such as the PNCC faces some obvious problems in this country during the next 50 years. Already many Protestant churches, especially the Lutheran churches, have quietly dropped their distinctively national names, languages, and appeals.

The original bone of contention, lay control of church property, seems as dead an issue as any in American Catholic life. Although Roman Catholic laymen have assumed positions of responsibility undreamed of in 1895, no one seriously questions the basic wisdom of the Baltimore decision on title to church property.

Language served as another plank in the PNCC platform of protest. Today the vernacular has been introduced into the Catholic sacraments of Baptism, Matrimony, and Extreme Unction. Most liturgists expect a wider use of English in place of Latin in the Mass and Holy Week services as a result of the decisions of the Second Vatican Council.

When the original schisms erupted, the Poles in America could count no one of their number in the American hierarchy. Today a Polish-American serves as Archbishop of Philadelphia and names such as Atkielski, Bona, Noa, Klonowski, Wosnicki, and Zaleski adorn the list of bishops in the United States. We estimate at least

2000 American priests of Polish nationality and 7000 nuns. In the Polish homeland it is clear to all that it is the Roman Catholic Church and its valiant Cardinal Wyszynski which uphold true Polish nationalism, while the Russian masters manipulate the PNCC.

The specific complaints of the disaffected Polish Catholics at the turn of the century were things which time would have taken care of. The bishops, Irish or not, were not opposed to the preservation of Polish culture but to the theory that the future of Americans of Polish (or any other) descent lay in isolation from the rest of the community.

Andrews observes:

> The Polish National Catholic Church exemplifies the language-bond, national (i.e., Polish) spirit, and property-hunger of Polish immigrants: all fundamental ideas in the mind of its founder, Francis Hodur. The lessening of immigrations, and the rapid adaptation of the younger generation to American ways, have profoundly modified the outlook of Polish-Americans; so that the concept of a Church whose mission is to lead a crusade for the redemption of Polish people through a religious body under their own control seems less compelling than of old (p. 14).

We wonder what the young PNCC member who knows only a smattering of Polish thinks about the completely Polish liturgy? We wonder if the German-American or Italian-American wife or husband of a PNCC member would care to affiliate with a sect so thoroughly nationalistic. We wonder if the PNCC begins to serve the religious needs of a people who, along with the rest of American society, are increasingly mobile. Outside of a few states they would find no PNCC parishes at all. We wonder if the average member has the slightest concern about who holds title to the church building.

Unlike a similar schism, the Philippine Independent Church or Aglipayans, the PNCC may well hold valid orders through Old Catholic sources. They may even succeed in reintroducing the apostolic succession into Anglicanism. With closer contact with Anglicanism and the ecumenical movement, the present PNCC hierarchy may be able to discard or reinterpret some of the unorthodoxies of the Hodur era.

One indication of a new, more orthodox attitude is given in a recent action by Prime Bishop Grochowski. Originally a Catholic priest, Joseph Alen had joined the PNCC and been appointed pastor of a parish in South Deerfield, Mass. His growing unorthodoxy prompted Bishop Grochowski to ask for his resignation. He left the PNCC in 1955 and took a number of parishioners with him into the Unitarian fold. Under the first Prime Bishop, Alen might have continued in the PNCC ministry despite his Unitarian tendencies.

What the bishops, priests, and faithful of the PNCC must ask themselves today is whether the causes of the original break are still serious enough to draw more than a quarter of a million Polish Americans from the faith of their fathers and to justify rending the Polish community. More sympathy and understanding on both sides might have averted the break; continued understanding and prayer will be the only means of healing the division in God's own time.

CHAPTER 16

THEOSOPHY AND THE LIBERAL CATHOLIC CHURCH

Madame Blavatsky Spins an Occult Web

———— • ————

Two women are immediately associated with the founding and spread of the occult concoction known as Theosophy: Madame Helena P. Blavatsky and Mrs. Annie Besant.

Madame Blavatsky, a Russian noblewoman, was born in South Russia in 1831 and even as a child was known as clairvoyant and psychic. She married Gen. N. V. Blavatsky at the age of 17, but left him after only two months and spent the next quarter of a century wandering throughout the world. She visited Paris, London, Greece, Egypt, India, South America, and the United States.

She became a spiritualist medium and eventually claimed to have received special revelations from mysterious Masters or Mahatmas. These Masters were supposedly men who were eligible to reach the blissful state of Nirvana but chose to remain in human bodies in order to assist man in his spiritual evolution. They were said to live for hundreds of years and to reside in remote regions of Tibet, China, India, Syria, and the Far East.

Joined by a former Civil War colonel and lawyer, Henry S. Olcott, Madame Blavatsky founded the Theosophical Society in New York City in 1875. She went to India and her society became markedly anti-Christian: "The Theosophical Society means, if it cannot rescue Christians from modern Christianity, at least to aid in saving the 'heathen' from its influence." Madame Blavatsky borrowed freely from Buddhism, Hinduism, and Spiritualism and added liberal portions of the product of her own wild imagination. The

Theosophical Society turned into a secret society with a degree system similar to that of Freemasonry.

The Society for Psychic Research investigated Madame Blavatsky while she was living in India and declared that she was "one of the most accomplished, ingenious and interesting imposters in history."

Belief in the existence of the Masters is basic in Theosophy. There are said to be 50 or 60 such Masters of whom two, Master Morya and Master Serapis, were instrumental in founding the Society. Below them in the occult hierarchy are the Arhats, the initiates of the three degrees of Theosophy, and finally the chelas or novices.

Madame Blavatsky wrote several of the basic texts of the movement including *The Secret Doctrine* and *Isis Unveiled*. Fr. C. C. Martindale, S.J., a student of occultism, has written: "Her information was encyclopaedic, but altogether confused, always inaccurate, often entirely misleading, and wholly at the mercy of her riotous imagination and unscrupulous methods."

Relations cooled between the Madame and the Colonel and she withdrew from an active role in the Theosophical Society to direct a secret Esoteric Society in London. Under the leadership of William Q. Judge the American branch withdrew from the world movement in 1895.

Madame Blavatsky died in 1891 and Colonel Olcott died in 1907. Mrs. Annie Besant (1847–1933) assumed control of the Theosophical Society. Mrs. Besant had married an Anglican clergyman, divorced him, lost her faith in Christianity, embraced atheism, and finally had fallen under the spell of Theosophy. When Madame Blavatsky died she claimed the right of succession and produced a green ring given to her by the Madame as proof of her claims. She moved to India where she became active in Indian politics and the independence movement, becoming president of the Indian National Congress in 1917. Mrs. Besant founded a college of Theosophy which became the University of Benares; money rolled in from wealthy patrons. Eventually she won the allegiance of most English, Indian, and Dutch theosophists.

An ex-medium, Mrs. Katherine Tingley, took over control of the independent American branch when Judge died. She declared that she was the "Purple Mother" of Theosophical mythology and founded the Point Loma Theosophical Community in San Diego, California. Starting with a gift of 40 acres she acquired 450 more acres and built 40 buildings. Largest of these was The Homestead, a residence with 90 rooms and a green glass dome. A uniformed bugler announced visitors to the nearby Aryan Temple with a toot on his horn. Some 300 initiates from 25 countries turned over their money to Mrs. Tingley and lived at The Homestead. Mrs. Tingley lived with her dog Spot, the reincarnation of the favorite of her three former husbands. Visitors flocked to the center to watch plays in the 2500-seat Greek theater and attend discussions at the lyceum.

Annie Besant carried on a feud with Mrs. Tingley for years. She carried the fight to California when she acquired a temple and vegetarian cafeteria in Hollywood. The two Theosophical rivals issued derogatory statements about each other and both bid for the loyalty of Madame Blavatsky's students.

Annie played a trump card when she adopted an Indian lad by the name of Krishnamurti and declared he was the reincarnation of Christ. He was the messiah the world was waiting for and would preside over a new race of enlightened mortals in California. Krishnamurti traveled throughout Europe with Mrs. Besant and arrived in New York in 1926 with the publicity treatment usually reserved for heads of state. He lectured in major American cities and was mobbed by members of the Order of the Star, Annie's American followers. Mrs. Tingley sniffed that the young man had been hypnotized by Mrs. Besant.

Annie revealed plans for a huge Theosophical colony in Ojai, California, which would put the Point Loma community to shame. But the Theosophical craze was petering out and in a few years both Mrs. Besant and Mrs. Tingley would have passed to their next reincarnation. Krishnamurti rejected his role as a modern messiah and retired in Ojai. He visits India once in a while. The Homestead went bankrupt and the remnant moved to Pasadena to carry on Mrs. Tingley's version of Theosophy.

Theosophy today is split into various sects with a world membership of perhaps 35,000 in 1300 lodges. Adyar, Madras, India, where the Society owns a 266-acre estate, is world headquarters. The movement operates in 80 nations. Wheaton, Illinois, is the center for the independent American movement. The smaller United Lodge of Theosophists and the Theosophical Society have centers in Los Angeles and Corina, California, respectively. The movement seems to be disintegrating, although the Wheaton group carries on publishing and missionary activities.

Theosophists teach that besides the material world there are six invisible worlds of subtle matter. These worlds interpenetrate the visible world as water interpenetrates a sponge. Man possesses three bodies: the physical body of activity, the astral body of emotion, and the mental body of thought.

Man is perfectible and passes through a series of reincarnations to rid himself of his impurities. The Buddhist law of Karma explains his misfortunes and sufferings in this life as the consequences of sins in a previous life. Man is ultimately responsible for whatever befalls him, even though he has no remembrance of previous existences. The cult's idea of God is thoroughly pantheistic.

Theosophical ideas have been picked up by such groups as the Rosicrucians, I Am, Unity School of Christianity, sections of the New Thought movement, and even by Father Divine's Peace Mission. Few of the dozens of Southern California cults do not owe a debt to Madame Blavatsky and her occult creation, Theosophy.

Oddest of the many offshoots of Theosophy is the Liberal Catholic Church, which attempts to blend Theosophy with Catholicism and which claims valid orders through the Old Catholic succession. The larger of the three Liberal Catholic factions in the United States claims eight churches and 4000 members.

Liberal Catholics trace their orders through Arnold Harris Mathew (1852–1919), an unstable character, more to be pitied than to be blamed, for even his enemies could not find anything with which to charge him except temperamental irresponsibility. He had been baptized by a Catholic priest in France where he was born, but was raised as an Anglican. Having studied for the ministry of the Scottish

Episcopal Church, he rejoined the Catholic Church at the age of 23.

He was rushed through his studies of philosophy and theology in eighteen months and awarded a Roman degree of Doctor of Divinity. Mathew was ordained a priest in 1877.

During the next twelve years Fr. Matthews (as he was then called) worked in five dioceses as a secular priest, was professed as a Dominican, and dispensed from his simple vows. In 1889 he became a Unitarian. Two years later he rejoined the Church of England, attempted marriage in 1892 (under the name of the Rev. Count Povoleri di Vicenza), changed his name from Matthews to Mathew, and styled himself de jure 4th Earl of Landaff of Thomastown, Co., Tipperary. The title had been considered extinct since 1833, and there is no evidence that his father ever tried to claim it.

After ministering as honorary curate at a London church for two or three years Mathew regained his faith in Catholicism. Having a wife and three children to support, all he could do was to lead the life of a layman. Between 1898 and 1908 he published many books, and his name appeared in the Catholic Who's Who. Then he suddenly developed a violent hatred of the papacy, and appealed to the Archbishop of Canterbury to find him clerical work in the Church of England, but without success. Encouraged by several lapsed Catholic priests and layfolk, some of them Modernists, and also a few disgruntled Anglicans, he got in touch with Old Catholic bishops in Holland and Switzerland, leading them to believe that he had a large following in England eager to cast off the yoke of the papacy.

On April 28, 1908, Mathew was raised to the episcopate by the Archbishop of Utrecht, and given the title of Regionary Old Catholic Bishop for England. Two years later he issued what he called a "Declaration of Autonomy and Independence," in which he accused the continental Old Catholics of having lapsed into heresy. Assuming the title of Archbishop of London he changed the name of his schismatic sect seven times in nine years — English Catholic Church, Western Orthodox Catholic Church in Great Britain and Ireland, Anglo-Catholic Church, Catholic Church (Latin and Orthodox United), Ancient Catholic Church, Old Roman Catholic Church, and Western Catholic Uniate Church. Between 1910 and 1916 he consecrated twelve or more bishops, two of them lapsed Catholic monsignori, and ordained a large number of priests.

By 1915 the greater number of his clergy were members of the Theosophical Society and the Order of the Star of the East. It seems that he was indifferent to their beliefs. In August that year he issued a Pastoral Letter, ordering his priests and layfolk to give up their Theosophical connections and to repudiate heresy. The result was that he found himself virtually alone. At the same time his wife sought a divorce which he refused to consider. In January, 1916, he announced that he was going to submit to the Roman Church, but he changed his mind after three months. During the next three years he tried again and again to obtain work in the Church of England, but none of the bishops would consider it. Archbishop Mathew died, near London, in 1919, and was buried with Anglican rites.

On October 28, 1914, Mathew had consecrated (after reordination) a former Anglican priest, Frederick Samuel Willoughby, who had been deposed for alleged immorality. A year later this titular Bishop of St. Pancras was expelled from Mathew's body, before performing any ordinations or consecrations. In 1915, Willoughby raised to the episcopate two Theosophist priests. In February, 1916, he consecrated James Ingall Wedgwood, who had been converted to Theosophy by Mrs. Besant in 1904, and subsequently ordained priest by Mathew. Wedgwood then went to Australia, where on July 22, 1916, he consecrated Charles W. Leadbeater, another ex-Anglican clergyman, who had been converted to Theosophy by Madame Blavatsky in the 1880's, and who had been closely connected with Mrs. Besant's movement in India. In 1918 the Theosophical section of Mathew's Old Roman Catholic Church — by this time far the largest group — was given the official title of the Liberal Catholic Church. Leadbeater was elected Presiding Bishop in 1923. He died in 1934.

Between 1916 and 1929, the Liberal Catholic Church was established in Europe, Australia, New Zealand, the East Indies, and North America. Regionary Bishops, with the rank of Archbishops, were appointed as heads of Provinces, ruling over Suffragans who were equivalent to diocesan bishops, with Auxiliaries to assist them.

Irving Steiger Cooper was made Regionary Bishop for America in 1919 and by 1925 he was able to dedicate St. Alban's Procathedral in Los Angeles.

Few of the so-called Old Catholic Churches either in Europe or in North America can claim that they carried on for nearly thirty years without one or more schisms, which was the case with the Liberal Catholic Church; all the more remarkable because its members can believe almost anything they like. During World War II difficulties arose in the United States Province, due in the first instance to the independent line of action adopted by Charles Hampton, who had been consecrated in 1931 as Auxiliary Bishop for the United States.

At the present time there are three distinct groups of Liberal Catholics in North America. Those who recognize the authority of the Presiding Bishop, Adriaan G. Vreede, whose residence is in Holland, have Newton A. Dahl as their Regionary Bishop. His headquarters are at Minneapolis, and he has three episcopal assistants. In recent years this body has spread to Central and South America, where Provinces have been erected.

In 1961, after some years of litigation, the Supreme Court of California gave judgment that the only *legal* Liberal Catholic Church was the group under Bishop Edward M. Matthews, which has its headquarters at Los Angeles, with Suffragan Bishops resident in New York and in Ontario, Canada. Linked up with this body is a schismatic group which broke away from the Liberal Catholic Church in Europe in 1959.

Then there is another neo-Theosophical sect — The Church Universal — whose first bishop, Hermann S. Spruit, a former Methodist minister, was consecrated by Bishop Hampton in 1957, after he had been deposed by the Presiding Bishop of the Liberal Catholic Church. It is now known as the Christian Catholic Church, and its headquarters are at Downey, California.

Not all Liberal Catholics are Theosophists, and certainly not all Theosophists are Liberal Catholics, but the connection between the two has persisted since the times of Wedgwood-Leadbeater. As late as 1933 the Liberal Catholic bishop for India was elected president of the world Theosophical society.

Liberal Catholics are found in England, Germany, Canada, Cuba, Australia, Yugoslavia, New Zealand, Holland, and the United States. World headquarters are in London.

Congregations are small and often the chapel is simply the living room or front porch of the local priest. Attendance of 50 or 60 people would delight the pastor even on Christmas eve. Many of the male devotees are priests or deacons which enables the parish to hold elaborate solemn high Masses and liturgical functions.

The consecration of a new bishop at St. Michael's Center in Huizen, Holland, attracted 80 Liberal Catholic priests and bishops and nearly 500 people in 1962. Clergy attended from Austria, Belgium, Denmark, France, England, Germany, Holland, Norway, Sweden, and the United States.

The Liberal Catholic Church, Province of the U.S.A., recognizes 25 parishes, missions, and church centers. The Regionary Bishop in Minneapolis is also an organ architect. The Auxiliary Bishop for New York is a retired chief engineer of the Municipal Broadcasting System of the City of New York and a naval reserve commander. He and his wife edit the quarterly magazine *Ubique*. The other two bishops live in Ann Arbor, Michigan, and Tulsa, Oklahoma. One is a doctor and the other a public accountant. The Presiding Bishop, Dr. Vreede, is a retired judge of the High Court of Indonesia.

In the statement of principles of the Los Angeles body we read: "It [the LCC] combines the Catholic form of worship — its stately ritual, its deep mysticism, and its abiding witness to the reality of sacramental grace — with the widest measure of intellectual liberty and respect for the individual conscience." It adds "The Liberal Catholic Church permits to lay members entire freedom in the interpretation of Creeds, Scriptures and Traditions, and of the Liturgy. It asks only that differences of interpretation be courteously expressed." In other words, the Liberal Catholic can believe whatever he wishes while participating in the "Mass" and other traditional Catholic devotions and sacraments.

Its ritual follows the Roman rite but is in the vernacular. "The fear of God's wrath, the attitude of abject self-abasement, together with the haunting fear of eternal hell, have been eliminated from the ritual," explains the statement of principles. No crucifixes or other representations of the dead Christ are allowed in Liberal Catholic churches.

Auricular confessional is optional and frequent confession is discouraged. Absolution may also be given after a general silent confession. Priests may marry. They may not accept fees for their spiritual services.

The Liberal Catholic Church believes that other world religions besides Christianity are divinely inspired. Therefore it makes no attempt to convert adherents of other religions. The Christ principle, it holds, has appeared many times in history in human form to found the higher religions. Jesus was one such manifestation of this Christ principle.

The Liberal Catholic bishop of New York has said that any study of comparative religion shows, "present-day orthodox Christianity, whether Catholic or Protestant, to be far inferior to some other faiths in sublimity of teaching, in breadth of vision, and above all in concept of the nature of God and His plan and purpose regarding life in general and humanity in particular."

Man dies and is reborn again and again in reincarnations. The Liberal Catholic Church denies the existence of hell and considers purgatory simply the time and place between reincarnations. The Eastern doctrine of Karma, adopted by Theosophy, has also been taken over by the Liberal Catholics.

Reincarnation presents Liberal Catholics with many opportunities for speculation. They believe that the dead return as babies among their former friends and relatives. The September, 1961, issue of *Ubique* carried the following item: "In various places throughout the world the new babies are returning to incarnation in Liberal Catholic families, and in these places many of us are playing the 'Who is it?' guessing game — wondering just which one of the old workers this or that baby might be" (p. 55). An infant or child who dies is thought to return as another baby to the same parents. A man may live hundreds of lives, one after another, starting as a savage until he finally achieves the life which allows him to follow in the footsteps of Christ.

Spiritual healing is also emphasized. The means used are holy unction, absolution, and the sacred oil for the sick. The LCC book of liturgy presents a detailed healing service. Liberal Catholics also patronize regular physicians.

The Liberal Catholic magazine *Ubique* describes a recent healing service in Holland. For this service the altar is decorated in green, "the healing color." Each participant lights a candle and offers it, making a strong mental picture of the sick person as he gazes through the flame. "The influence of this service is quite perceptible to a sensitive person."

A real belief in spirits and ghosts pervades the Liberal Catholic movement. One bishop relates such a psychic experience in the June, 1962, issue of *Ubique*. Turning to give the general absolution to the congregation at Mass, he says he "sensed the indubitable presence of 15 Navy officers and men, dressed in spotless white uniform, standing quietly, attentively, questioningly perhaps, just beyond the communion rail — the crew of a giant dirigible which had crashed into the ocean a day or so previously. Suddenly transferred from this world to the next, they seemed to sense that in this service, to which they had of course been invited, they might find help and direction in the new life facing them."

Again the same bishop relates the plight of a Liberal Catholic priest who was pestered by a ghost in his house. These ghosts are the spirits of irreligious people who find themselves dead and do not understand their situation. "They see their old surroundings and their old acquaintances, who, however, cannot see them and so pay no attention to them, so, they are very much bewildered." The bishop hesitated to perform the exorcism until the priest had tried to enlighten his ghostly visitor. He advised the priest:

> Next time you feel the ghost around, talk to him just as though he were a living person there present. Tell him you know he is there tho you can't see him nor hear him, but you know he sees you and hears you. Tell him that he is dead — he may not

realize it — and that you want to help him. Tell him something about the "astral" world he is now living in and how to get along in it, how to turn his thoughts away from the material world towards the higher world. Invite him to come with you to church on Sunday, and remember him in your prayers. Let him know that you are his friend and want to help him. Tell him to ask questions, thinking very hard about them, and maybe you will get his thought and can give the answers. Whenever any such "question" enters your mind, give the answer just as you would to a living person. Let me know what happens; and if this does not improve matters, we shall see about an exorcism.

This evidently worked. The priest had a few chats with the ghost and explained the facts of death to him and the ghost went away.

Neither Theosophy nor its Liberal Catholic stepchild seems to have much of a future. In most countries they appear to be losing rather than gaining members, a situation which is not likely to be reversed. The death of the original Theosophists — Blavatsky, Olcott, Besant, Leadbeater — left the movement bereft of dynamic leadership. As might be expected, schisms and feuds have rent the tiny cult, simply because one of its principles is "the widest measure of intellectual liberty and respect for the individual conscience." What this amounts to in the long run is that a Liberal Catholic can believe anything he likes, and still be a good one. Persons of any religion or none are allowed to receive the sacraments, and no priest has the right to refuse them.

CHAPTER 17

AGLIPAYANISM

Philippine Independent Church
Broke From Rome in 1902

———— • ————

Recent reports indicate that Fidel Castro plans to set up a national Catholic church in Cuba to serve the objectives of his revolution. Red China has severed all contact between the Chinese hierarchy and Rome and uses "patriotic" priests and bishops to staff the schismatic Chinese church.

Even in the United States a group of disaffected Polish Catholics around the turn of the century established the schismatic Polish National Catholic Church. National churches have sprung up in Czechoslovakia, Brazil, and Mexico. None of them has prospered.

These national churches are nothing new. They have plagued the Church since her earliest days. Many have died with the deaths of their founders while others, such as the Church of England, have survived for hundreds of years. Typically they pass from schism to heresy.

One of the few successful modern schisms is the Philippine Independent Church (*Iglesia Filipina Independiente*) whose 1961 official directory claims 2,781,984 members. It is also known as the Aglipayan Church. This body forms the largest Christian communion in the Far East outside the Roman Catholic Church; however, the PIC statistics are inflated. When the results of the 1960 census are published in full it would appear that the total number of Aglipayans will be closer to 1,400,000 in the main church and eight others originating in the Aglipayan schism.

Founded in the turmoil of the Philippine Revolution and the

American occupation in 1902, the PIC drifted into unitarianism until the death of Gregorio Aglipay and the succession of Isabelo de los Reyes, Jr., as Supreme Bishop in 1946. Two years later the Protestant Episcopal Church bestowed what it believed to be the apostolic succession and valid orders. Full intercommunion between the two churches was achieved in 1961.

Currently the PIC reports 390 parishes in cities and towns in the Islands, about 2000 chapels in the barrios and rural areas, 425 priests, and 38 bishops. The total population of the Philippines stands at approximately 27 million. Of these four out of five are baptized Roman Catholics.

The standard Catholic reference books are outdated or misleading when it comes to discussing Aglipayanism. For example, the *Catholic Concise Encyclopedia*, published in 1957, tells us "Aglipay died reconciled to the Church, in September, 1940. The movement is now minor and has but few followers in the Islands" (p. 24). The fact is that Aglipay died an Aglipayan. This is confirmed by all authorities including the two Jesuits, Frs. Pedro S. de Achutegui and Miguel A. Bernad, who have written the history of the movement, *Religious Revolution in the Philippines*.

The *Catholic Encyclopedia* states: "With the restoration of the churches under orders of the Supreme Court in 1906–07, the schism began to dwindle, and its adherents are now inconsiderable" (Vol. 12, p. 16).

Finally, Konrad Algermissen in *Christian Denominations*, concludes that the Aglipayan schism "dwindled rapidly in the ensuing years (after 1918) to 100,000 members, and is dissolving more and more as a result of the new religious fervor that has been engendered by the International Eucharistic Congress held in Manila in 1937" (pp. 364–365).

The facts of the situation are quite different from these sanguine estimates and predictions. A claimed constituency of more than 2½ million souls cannot be reckoned as minor or inconsiderable. The PIC has finally jettisoned the unitarianism which infected Aglipay and some of the church leaders. At least since 1947 this church has subscribed to as orthodox a Trinitarian position as, say, Anglicanism.

The PIC not only enjoys the moral and financial support of the Philippine Episcopal Church, a missionary district of the Episcopal Church in the United States, but holds full membership in the World Council of Churches. Its seminarians form the majority of the 100 students at St. Andrew's Theological Seminary in Quezon City. It is publishing a new missal, liturgy, and book of divine worship, and has even sent two missionaries to work among the Filipinos in Hawaii.

Unlike some national churches, the PIC has never possessed valid orders. No bishops participated in the original revolt and Aglipay did not succeed in obtaining consecration from the Old Catholics or Orthodox. He and the other PIC bishops were simply consecrated by each other. Of course, the Catholic Church does not recognize the Anglican orders which PIC bishops now possess any more than Anglicans recognize the orders of Methodists or Presbyterians.

Like every successful revolt since Lutheranism, the Aglipayans seized on the popularity of a vernacular liturgy to win the people. The PIC uses local vernaculars wherever possible and also prints official documents in English. Priests and bishops may marry. Communion is distributed under both species. Church externals differ little from Catholic churches: Aglipayan chapels include tabernacles, crucifixes, statues of the Blessed Virgin Mary and saints, stations of the cross. Auricular confession is rare; usually the Aglipayan priest pronounces absolution after the penitent makes a silent confession before the altar.

To understand the background of the PIC we must take a brief look at the religious history of the Islands. For 300 years the Spanish ruled the Philippines. During these centuries practically all ecclesiastical positions were held by members of the Spanish religious orders. Little effort was made to develop a native clergy, much less a native Filipino hierarchy. Four religious orders — the Augustinians, Franciscans, Dominicans, and Augustinian Recollects — dominated the religious life of the islands.

Today the Philippines is represented in the College of Cardinals but up to 1900 not a single Filipino had been consecrated a bishop nor been given any responsible post in the Church. Native priests served only as curates in parishes administered by the Spanish friars.

Resentment against the friars was widespread among both the laity and secular clergy. The patriot-novelist Jose Rizal expressed much of this bitterness in his popular books. (He and three other patriots have been canonized by the PIC.)

Two men stand out in the founding of the PIC: Isabelo de los Reyes, Sr., and Gregorio Aglipay. Don Isabelo (1864–1938) was a journalist, labor leader, senator, and businessman as well as an amateur theologian. Widely read, he was influenced by free thought, Masonry, and paganism. When the authorities accused him of involvement in the Katipunan revolt in 1896 he was deported to Spain but was released in the general amnesty the next year.

The elder de los Reyes married three wives and outlived them all. He had 28 children, including three who are Roman Catholic nuns, one who married a Japanese woman and embraced Shintoism, and Isabelo de los Reyes, Jr., the present head of the PIC.

The insurrection sparked by the Katipunan revolt continued throughout the Islands and Emilio Aguinaldo seized control of the Filipino forces and was proclaimed head of the Revolutionary government. But now a new element enters the picture. The United States declared war on Spain and ordered Admiral Dewey to destroy the Spanish navy in the Philippines. On May 1, 1898, Dewey's fleet entered Manila Bay and by midnight the same day the Spanish fleet was annihilated. Soon, except for Manila itself and a few other cities, the entire archipelago was in control of Filipino forces. Aguinaldo sought independence for the Philippines rather than a transfer of authority from one foreign power to another. In this he would be disappointed.

Fr. Gregorio Aglipay's sympathy for the Filipino forces under Aguinaldo was well known. His objective at this time was to see an independent Philippines with a union of Church and State which would force the friars out and provide for native bishops and pastors.

Aglipay was born on May 5, 1860, in Ilocos in the northwestern part of Luzon. His mother died when he was an infant. He received a B.A. degree from the University of Santo Tomas, run by the

Dominicans, and entered the seminary at Vigan. He was not a model seminarian but was transferred from his native diocese of Nueva Segovia to the archdiocese of Manila and was ordained in 1889. During the next eight years Fr. Aglipay was assigned to various parishes.

His friendship with the rebels prompted General Aguinaldo to appoint him military chaplain. On October 20, 1898, Aguinaldo promoted Fr. Aglipay to the post of Military Vicar General. Aglipay considered himself "spiritual head of a nation under arms" and a few days after his appointment he asked the clergy to renounce their allegiance to the Spanish hierarchy and to elect an all-Filipino church organization. He reasoned that the incumbent bishops were appointed through the Spanish government and received their salaries from Spain. When Spain was driven out of the Islands, Aglipay maintained that the Spanish bishops lost their authority. He was confusing the religious and political orders.

On April 29, 1899, the archbishop of Manila excommunicated Fr. Aglipay for usurping ecclesiastical power and other offenses. Aglipay called for a convention of sympathetic Filipino priests at Paniqui on October 23, 1899. Twenty-seven priests attended and signed what amounted to a declaration of independence from the existing hierarchy. At this time the movement intended to continue to recognize the authority of the Pope.

Soon after this meeting the American forces advanced into the interior and the Filipino army was disbanded. The Revolutionary government decided to continue its opposition to the American occupation by guerrilla tactics. Plans to implement the decisions at Paniqui were shelved as Aglipay donned the uniform of a guerrilla general. His men harassed the American army and a price of 50,000 pesos was put on his head. He was the last guerrilla general to surrender on May 1, 1901.

Not Aglipay but Isabelo precipitated the actual formation of a schismatic church in a widely advertized speech to his labor union in 1902. "I solemnly declare that today we definitely secede from the Church of Rome, and renounce allegiance to the Vatican, and . . . proclaim ourselves members of a Christian, Catholic, and Independent Church." His speech called on Aglipay to head the new church as its supreme bishop but Aglipay hesitated to take this step. He began a retreat with the Jesuits at Santa Ana but did not come back to the Church. Instead he yielded to Isabelo's pleas and became supreme bishop of the Philippine Independent Church in September, 1902.

Aglipay was "consecrated" by a number of fellow schismatic priests on January 18, 1903. He realized that he would have to justify this action since even a poorly instructed Filipino would know that a priest could not "consecrate" a bishop. He advanced five reasons why bishops could be consecrated by priests. First, the apostles themselves did not prescribe a ritual. Second, the apostles were not consecrated by a bishop. Third, Jesus Christ was a bishop and all priests are His representatives. Fourth, there is no distinction of orders between a bishop and a priest. Fifth, in case of necessity a layman can baptize so in other cases of necessity priests should be able to consecrate bishops.

The early and rapid success of the movement cannot be disputed. The attraction of an all-Filipino church appealed to many patriots who disliked both the Spanish friars and the Americans. Frs. Achutegui and Bernad state: "The Aglipayan movement initially was not a revolt against the Catholic Church as such but against a socio-political order of things in which the Catholic Church, as an external organization, was involved. The chief target was the nationality of the existing hierarchy" (p. 235).

They add: "The role of Freemasonry in adding fuel to the already existing fire cannot be overestimated" (p. 154). A similar judgment has been made by the Episcopalian Bishop Lewis Bliss Whittemore: "Masonry had become strong in the Islands. Emanating from Spain, it was of the Latin variety and therefore strongly anti-Catholic. It had played its part in revolutionary days and now it helped create a climate of opinion helpful to the (PI) Church which was independent of Rome" (*Struggle for Freedom*, p. 127). Aglipay joined the lodge himself in 1918 and later took the degrees of the Scottish Rite.

William Howard Taft, governor of the Islands, seemed to favor the schism and helped propel it into the paths of Unitarianism. At the same time he was suspicious of Aglipay and declined to accept the honorary presidency of the schismatic body. Taft proclaimed the doctrine of "peaceable possession" which enabled the schismatics to claim many former Catholic church buildings.

Finally, the large-scale religious invasion of the Philippines by Protestant missionaries from the United States helped undermine the Catholic faith of the people and spade the soil for Aglipayanism as well as Protestantism. The Presbyterians, Episcopalians, Disciples, Congregationalists, Baptists, and others arrived on the scene and in 1901 they assigned various territories among themselves. Manila was open to all denominations. Except for the Episcopalians who labored among the Moslems and pagans, the other churches and sects sought to win converts among the traditionally Catholic population.

By 1904 the PIC probably enrolled 1,500,000 of the Islands' seven million people. About 50 priests joined Aglipay in the new church. Its further growth was hampered by the Supreme Court decisions which in 1906–1907 stripped the PIC of the Catholic property it had acquired through "peaceable possession." The United States Supreme Court upheld the decision in 1909.

The PIC had to abandon these facilities and attempt to build new churches and chapels for its adherents. Aglipay visited Bishop Charles Brent of the Protestant Episcopal Church but the two men did not get along. He corresponded with the Swiss Old Catholic bishop but the latter was suspicious of the unitarian tendencies of the new church.

Bishop Whittemore reveals that Don Miguel Morayta, Grand Master of the Spanish Orient, was urging Aglipay to obtain valid consecration from the Old Catholics or Orthodox as the only way to compete with the Roman Church (p. 137).

Don Isabelo remained the man behind the throne and the church's leading layman. He composed all the church's doctrinal works although Aglipay's name appeared on the title pages. The Jesuit historians point out: "There is a certain lack of logic in this name [Aglipayan] for it was Isabelo de los Reyes who formally launched the schism and gave it its organizational structure, its doctrine, and its liturgy. But Isabelo de los Reyes, while being the moving spirit behind the scenes, hid himself behind the mantle of the 'Obispo Maximo'" (p. 210).

Isabelo's views were rationalistic. He pronounced the idea of original sin absurd. The manhood of Jesus was only an illusion. There was no atonement. There is no heaven or hell after this life.

A professor at St. Andrew's Seminary describes the early theological formation of the PIC:

> Among those who were deeply interested in the Independent Church was Wm. H. Taft. The leaders of the Church responded to his friendship, and under Taft's leadership, the teachings of unitarianism were brought to bear on Aglipay and several of the Independiente leaders. Unitarian doctrines began to be reflected in the statements of these leaders. The *Oficio Divino*, printed in Spain and adopted as an official book of the Church in 1906, was a reformed liturgy, strongly unitarian in tone, denying several important catholic teachings, while adhering closely to the external forms of catholic services. Unitarianism never infiltrated deeply into the thought of the Church, however, and remained a surface influence, the rank and file of the clergy and people remaining orthodox in belief (H. Ellsworth Chandlee, *Diocesan Chronicle of the Philippine Episcopal Church*, August, 1960, p. 5).

Catholic students of the movement would say that Chandlee exaggerates the influence of Taft and his friendship for Aglipay. They would see the hand of Isabelo in the new church's doctrinal shifts.

The *Oficio Divino* was written by Isabelo in Spain and published in Barcelona. Part I is a free translation of the Gospel of St. Mark. Part II is an explanation of the true meaning of the eucharist which the author obtained by visiting numerous Christian churches as well as Brahmin and Buddhist temples! Part III consists of ceremonial instructions. "There can be no doubt that in publishing the *Oficio Divino* and in forcing it upon the Aglipayan hierarchy, Isabelo de los Reyes was forcing the sect to accept his own rationalistic and anti-Christian ideas" (Acheteguí and Bernad, p. 262).

Whittemore explains that Aglipay moved farther into the unitarian camp after 1920: "In these new manifestos Aglipay really did away with the *Oficio Divino*, just as the latter had superseded the

Fundamental Epistles. Jesus was now just a man, a very good man to be sure, but that was all. The last and greatest miracle, the Incarnation, had disappeared. The Mass became just a brotherly meal" (p. 144).

At a public meeting in 1930 Bishop Aglipay asserted: "The existence of a God with three distinct persons and the pretended submission of God to the will of a man invested with priestly character to convert into God a piece of bread called a host, are absurdities which the human mind, illumined by reason, rejects."

American Unitarians saw in the PIC an opportunity to transplant Unitarianism to the Islands in a ready-made vehicle. The Unitarians paid the expenses of Aglipay, Isabelo de los Reyes, and Santiago Fonacier on a tour of the United States in 1931. Aglipay preached in Unitarian churches in St. Paul, Detroit, Toledo, Boston, New York, Philadelphia, Washington, D. C., Cleveland, and St. Louis. He attended the annual convention of the American Unitarian Association in Boston and his church was admitted into the International Association of Liberal Christianity. He obtained an interview with President Hoover and tried to plump for Philippine independence on every occasion.

A few years later Aglipay and the younger Isabelo went to the meeting of the International Association of Liberal Christianity in Copenhagen. They went by way of the United States and also visited Paris, Madrid, Rome, and other European cities. In St. Peter's a Spanish friar thought Aglipay was a genuine bishop because of his robes and asked if he might make his confession. Aglipay obliged and then revealed his identity.

Aglipay addressed the Copenhagen meeting in Tagalog and was hailed as the "Father of Religious Liberalism in the Orient." He was received by the king of Denmark.

Don Isabelo ran for the legislature again in 1934. A rift developed between himself and Aglipay when the latter also decided to enter the political arena. Isabelo had shown signs of mellowing in his opposition to the Catholic Church, sending all his children to Catholic schools and having many of them rebaptized Catholics. In 1934 he asked a priest to enthrone the Sacred Heart in his home.

Finally on September 14, 1936, he invited Fr. Louis Morrow to come to his home where he signed a recantation, made his confession, and was given absolution. Fr. Morrow is now Bishop of Krishnaga, India. Eight witnesses signed the recantation, including several of his children. Isabelo de los Reyes, Jr., and another son, Jose, the Shintoist and his biographer, deny the validity of the recantation as do most Aglipayans and Episcopalians. Nevertheless Isabelo lived for two years after his return to the church and received the sacraments regularly and finally extreme unction. He died on October 10, 1938. To avoid incidents two funeral services were held, one a requiem Mass and the other presided over by Aglipay. After World War II Isabelo de los Reyes, Jr., exhumed his father's body and reburied it in an Aglipayan church next to that of his mother and Aglipay.

The 75-year-old Aglipay ran for president in 1935 against Quezon and his old comrade, Aguinaldo. He polled 147,951 votes or 14 percent of the total.

In 1939 the president of the American Unitarian Association, the Rev. Louis Cornish, visited Aglipay. In one service in an Aglipayan church the old bishop put his robe and pectoral cross on his guest. Cornish was also invited to impose his hands in consecration of an apostate priest as "bishop." Aglipay proclaimed Cornish an Honorary President of the PIC.

Bishop Aglipay finally got married in 1939 at the age of 78. His wife, Miss Pilar Jamias, was 14 years his junior. His illegitimate daughter had died the year before at the age of 24. Born February 24, 1913, she had been a student at the University of the Philippines where she was generally known as Aglipay's daughter. Her tombstone in the cemetery in Pasay reads "Liwliwa J. Aglipay." Mr. and Mrs. Cornish were official witnesses to Aglipay's wedding.

Aglipay died on September 1, 1940. His body lay in state for two weeks in the PIC cathedral in Tondo. The present Supreme Bishop preached the eulogy. His body was interred in the PIC church in his hometown of Batac.

Achutegui and Bernad declare: "Aglipay died as he lived: an Aglipayan and Unitarian. There is no evidence of any reconciliation with the Catholic Church, and he did not die with the Catholic sacraments" (p. 516).

Bishop Fonacier was elected to succeed Aglipay but was deposed in 1946 and began a rival sect. Since 1950 he has had no formal connection with any Aglipayan church. Other Aglipayan factions besides the main PIC church include the Old Aglipayans, the Independent Church of Filipino Christians, the Philippine Unitarian Church, and the Filipino Christian Church.

The present Supreme Bishop, Isabelo de los Reyes, Jr., was born in Madrid in 1900. He attended a Catholic grade school in Barcelona, the Jesuit seminary college at Vigan, and the Ateneo de Manila. He completed part of his senior year of high school. Young Isabelo then joined the U. S. Navy for a four-year hitch and sailed around the world. In 1923 he returned to the Philippines, was tutored in theology by Bishop Aglipay, and ordained the same year. His secular and theological educations could hardly be more limited, but he is shrewd and possesses considerable administrative talent.

He was consecrated a bishop at the age of 25. The Supreme Bishop is married and has ten children, including two sons studying for the Aglipayan priesthood at St. Andrew's.

Bishop de los Reyes has abandoned his Unitarianism and brought the official position of the PIC back to fundamental Trinitarianism. He approached the Episcopalians to obtain the Anglican succession. In 1948 in the procathedral of St. Luke in Manila, three Protestant Episcopal bishops consecrated de los Reyes and two other PIC bishops. They reconsecrated the other PIC bishops and reordained all Aglipayan priests and deacons. These actions, of course, contradicted Aglipay's specious arguments to justify his own "consecration" at the hands of fellow apostate priests. Obviously a true apostolic succession was lacking and despite the Anglican attempt to remedy this deficiency the Catholic Church must still regard the Aglipayan bishops and priests as laymen in cassocks and miters, except for about 15 ex-Roman Catholic priests.

Now the PIC has obtained a concordat between itself and the Episcopal Church. Bishop de los Reyes attended the General Convention in Detroit which ratified the 1961 agreement. Two Episcopalian seminaries conferred honorary doctorates on the Obispo Maximo.

Each church involved in the concordat remains independent but each admits members of the other communion to the sacraments. Such a concordat is similar to that between the Protestant Episcopal Church and the Old Catholics of Europe and the Polish National Catholics.

Admittance of PIC seminarians to St. Andrew's is bound to strengthen the schismatic body. Over the years the PIC established a number of seminaries but all were disbanded. They relied on the tutorial system which was often sketchy and superficial. Since 1948 PIC candidates have enrolled at St. Andrew's for the regular five-year course and the short course. The Episcopal Church pays the tuition and even buys cassocks for the PIC seminarians. Now that intercommunion has been approved, scholarships and opportunities for foreign study may be forthcoming from Episcopalian funds.

Most of the PIC communicants have been drawn from the laboring and peasant classes. Bishop de los Reyes estimates that one out of five Aglipayans belongs to the middle class and only a handful are wealthy. Aglipayanism is weak in Manila. In seven provinces it claims 20 percent or more of the population. In 1948 Ilocos Norta was 59.7 percent Aglipayan, Zambales 37.8 percent, Misamis Occidental 37.1 percent, and Antique 30.7 percent.

The PIC operates no colleges of its own but maintains student foundations at secular universities. Most of its bishops are also tied down with parish duties and the church relies on a fee system for its support. Lt. Col. Benjamin Leano, president of the PIC Council of Bishops, is assistant chief of chaplains of the Philippine army.

In interviewing Bishop de los Reyes I asked him if his followers were sensitive to the Catholic charge that their newly acquired Anglican orders were invalid. He shrugged, "I ask my people if Anglicanism was good enough for Churchill, Roosevelt, and MacArthur, why should they worry if an Italian pope says these orders are invalid."

He acknowledged the support of Freemasonry and said that most of the bishops and priests of the PIC are Masons but he is not. "I do not have the time to be a Mason," he explained. At a Masonic banquet in Manila in 1958 the Supreme Bishop declared: "To them [the Freemasons], after God, we owe in great measure the existence of the Filipino Independent Church." He added, "The Iglesia Filipina Independiente is strong wherever Freemasonry is strong, and is weak wherever Freemasonry is weak."

The Supreme Bishop told me that where the Catholic Church had been served by faithful priests, Spanish or native, his church has been unable to gain a foothold. The PIC established itself in those cities and villages where the clergy exacted heavy church taxes and mistreated the people, he said.

"Our break with Rome would probably have been unnecessary under a pope such as the present one," he said. He remarked that his own PIC laity loved Pope John XXIII whom he called "everybody's favorite uncle." The Holy Father enjoys an immense popularity in the Philippines among all people, said the bishop.

The bishop considers himself a Catholic who can do without the pope. "Every night my family and I kneel to pray the rosary," he told me. The Mass he said which I witnessed was practically a Roman rite Mass in English with some additions from the Book of Common Prayer. It included the elevation of the host and chalice and the Last Gospel.

According to the liturgical books of the PIC the colors of the vestments are white, blue, and green — the colors of the Philippine flag. At the elevation of the Mass the worshipers are instructed to kneel to the strains of the national anthem.

Bishop de los Reyes reported that the long-standing animosity between Roman Catholics and Aglipayans disappeared during the hardships of the Japanese occupation. Incidents of violence are unknown. His church enjoys full religious freedom under the Philippine constitution.

No merger of the PIC and the Episcopal Church is contemplated. The tiny Episcopalian church in the Islands counts only 46,000 souls. It labors principally in the mountain province of northern Luzon.

The lesson of the need for a native clergy is illustrated by the tragic PIC schism. The Spanish friars had 300 years to develop a native clergy and hierarchy but they missed the opportunity. The situation changed especially after the Manila Council of 1907 and the growing vitality of the Catholic Church in the Philippines is admitted by all. Still only some 4000 priests are available to care for the spiritual needs of some 20 million Catholic Filipinos and more than half of these are missionaries from other countries.

Roman Catholics can rejoice that the present Supreme Bishop has at least brought the PIC back to an official trinitarian position. We would certainly prefer that men recognize the divinity of our Lord than deny it. Unfortunately, the intercommunion with the Protestant Episcopal Church will no doubt draw the PIC further from its Catholic heritage.

Once we have given the PIC the benefit of every doubt, we may be in a position to ask Bishop de los Reyes and his colleagues if they still believe that the religious situation in the Islands regarding the legitimate aspirations of the native clergy has not changed since 1902. Almost everyone thinks it has.

CHAPTER 18

ROSICRUCIANISM

*Mail Order Mysticism
Interests Many, Enrolls Few*

———— • ————

Every day hundreds of curious people respond to advertisements inserted in various periodicals by the Rosicrucians (AMORC) of San Jose, California. The full name of this cult is the Ancient and Mystical Order Rosae Crucis.

The ads promise that the Rosicrucian order can unlock the secret wisdom of the ages, banish fears and frustration, enrich the human spirit, and open the door to self-mastery. By writing a letter or postcard to the cult's headquarters the inquirer can take the first step toward a new life.

To disarm the religious person the ads emphatically state that the Rosicrucians are *not* a religious organization. The reader is assured that nothing in the Rosicrucian system will ever conflict with his own religious beliefs.

This worldwide advertizing campaign costs the AMORC more than $500,000 a year but it gets results. The cult mails out more than seven million letters, correspondence monographs, books, and brochures every year. The Rosicrucians must spread their nets wide since most inquirers go no further than the first mailing and the ranks of dues-paying members must be constantly replenished. Since devotees come and go the estimate of 60,000 active members at any one time may not be far off.

This commercial version of a centuries-old mystery school consists of a hodgepodge of Theosophy, reincarnation, superstition, Free-masonry, discarded scientific theories, phony Egyptology, vegetarianism, mental telepathy, and other occult borrowings. The package is purveyed to any who agree to contribute a $5 registration fee and $3.50 a month ad infinitum for two lessons a month, a magazine, and other "privileges" of membership.

The cult's basic appeal is to people of modest education and income who feel that others are succeeding while they are standing still or falling behind. The insecure come to believe that if only they could latch onto a secret key, they too could open the door to prosperity and peace of mind. This is what the attractive ads and booklets of the San Jose cult offer. Hundreds of thousands take the bait every year but few swallow the hook.

Millions of people of our day are looking for some magical method of self-mastery and material success. The well-to-do pay enormous fees to New York and Hollywood psychoanalysts. Others may turn to one of the many cults, such as I Am, Theosophy, the Unity School of Christianity, the Black Muslims, Christian Science, Baha'i, or Rosicrucianism. A few of these cults such as Unity and the AMORC masquerade as philosophical systems to deceive Christians into thinking they can combine Christianity and cultism.

Surrounding their activities with secrecy these cults not only provide an aura of mystery but allow the initiate to imagine that he knows things hidden from the great mass of lesser men. He may not hold an important job or college degree or have much money in the bank or social prestige but he is privy to wonderful arcana passed on through the ages from ancient Egyptian sages.

The current literature of the AMORC offers to develop will power, banish inferiority complexes, overcome bad habits, maintain health, reveal the secrets of reincarnation, attain "cosmic consciousness," disclose the true meaning of mystical symbols, etc., etc. All this requires no tedious study. It can be imparted to the select few in 60 or 90 minutes of reading a week in the privacy of their own homes. The cult suggests that students set aside one night a week, preferably Thursday, as lodge night for such study.

The inquirer receives a handsomely printed booklet entitled Mastery of Life. The accompanying sales letter and application blank explain the mechanics of joining the cult. The application asks for the usual vital statistics together with answers to certain questions such as "Will you consider with an open mind new ideas regarding life and the Universe?" It also asks the applicant if he believes in the existence of a "Supreme Being, Divine Mind, or God."

The applicant must also promise to keep confidential all reading material and lessons which he will receive in this "home study course in metaphysics and occultism." Apparently, if he shows these pages to his wife or Aunt Emma he will be violating his cosmic contract and the secret wisdom will lose its power.

Not many people who get the first mailing send in their $5 fee, and fewer still continue to contribute $42 a year to remain in good standing. Eventually the reluctant inquirers will get additional mailings over a period of weeks reminding them of the inestimable benefits of membership and finally offering a cut rate Associate Membership for only $1.50 a month. For this sum the Associate Member gets the monthly magazine, the *Rosicrucian Digest*, and his choice of any two lecture series from a list which includes "Numerology" and "Arcane Cosmology" which is defined as a "fascinating study of the theory that we live on the inside of the earth instead of on the outside." These second-class Rosicrucians do not become eligible to undergo the degree initiations, take the examinations, or participate in the rituals and special experiments which the $3.50 people enjoy.

(Inflation plagues the AMORC as it does other institutions. In 1939 full membership could be maintained for only $2 a month.)

Those who take the full membership become Grand Lodge Sanctum members which means that they are Rosicrucians by correspondence. They study the lessons in their homes and initiate themselves into the higher degrees. They stay in good standing as long as they continue to forward their dues to the treasurer in San Jose.

The Rosicrucian novice is urged to build a home altar consisting of a table, tablecloth, two candles, and a mirror. The cult's magazine in April, 1960, carried an ad for a love idol of an Egyptian princess which was recommended for the member's "private sanctum."

The official emblem of the AMORC is a gold cross with a single red rose in the center. The founder of the cult managed to obtain a United States patent on the device which he claimed was the only authentic Rosicrucian symbol. Variations of this emblem, including one with a garland of several roses, were adopted by other Rosicrucian sects.

The formula for the first-degree home initiation is fairly simple. The candidate stares at the mirror over his home altar and traces a five-inch cross on the glass while repeating "Hail, Rosy Cross." He concentrates for three minutes and then is instructed to place the tip of his left forefinger in the middle of his forehead and whisper "Peace." He is now a first-degree member.

He was supposed to have studied his lessons for six weeks before his initiation and he remains in the first degree for 12 more weeks. His monographs which the postman delivers describe special breathing exercises, mental vibrations, mystical comprehension, the life force, mystical centers of the brain, and attunement with others in distant places.

The novice spends another 12 weeks in the second degree and then advances to the third. It ordinarily takes between 9 and 12 months to complete Grand Lodge Sanctum membership. During these months the correspondence course is supplemented by simple science experiments such as you would find in a child's chemistry set. He learns how a magnet works, the structure of a crystal, the mechanics of blood circulation and digestion. All these elementary facts are colored by occult interpretations.

After reaching Grand Lodge Sanctum membership the Rosicrucian, like the Freemason, is encouraged to continue in the higher degrees. Nine Temple degrees follow the first three degrees. After receiving the Ninth Degree the Rosicrucian frater or soror may be invited to join the Illuminati, which is a society under the direction of the "Imperator and Personal Cosmic Masters."

Meanwhile the recruit is introduced to Rosicrucian health rules. He is told to face east as soon as he wakes up, inhale and exhale seven deep breaths, bathe, and drink a glass of water to start the day. He is told to eat meat sparingly if at all. Before meals the devout Rosicrucian will wash his hands, hold them palms downward over the food, and say a mental prayer. He learns to make a special sign of the cross. In court he is urged to take his oath not on the Bible but on the symbol of the Rosy Cross.

Grand Lodge Sanctum members may also attend regular Rosicrucian lodges in the larger cities and participate in the Egyptian-style initiations and rituals appropriate to their stage of mystical development. These lodges remind one of Masonic lodges as much of the lodge paraphernalia and ceremonies are obviously lifted from the Masonic work. To gain admittance to these lodges Rosicrucians must show a membership card and give the secret passwords. Active members of these lodges are known as Regional Lodge members; instead of reading the lessons in their homes they listen to them read in lodge meetings. They pay their dues to the local lodge which forwards a percentage of the income to San Jose.

A recent issue of the *Rosicrucian Digest* lists 100 regular lodges in 31 states, the District of Columbia, and Puerto Rico. California leads the list with 21 lodges followed by Texas with 11; Ohio, 6; and Puerto Rico, 6. Sixteen of these lodges own the regalia and equipment needed to perform the full-scale initiations for the 12 degrees.

France leads the list of foreign countries which support AMORC lodges with 26 lodges. Mexico and Venezuela have 13 each; Canada and Nigeria, 12 each; and Brazil, Cuba, and England, 11 each. Recently the author encountered several university students from Nigeria enrolled at a Big Ten university who were thoroughly committed to the fantasies of the Rosicrucian cult.

The Master of a Rosicrucian lodge sits on a triangular dias before a triangular lectern. Rosicrucian lodges, unlike Masonic lodges, are coeducational. The Matre of the lodge sits at the opposite end of the Chamber. Just in front of the Master's chair is the Vestal Colombe or Vestal Virgin who guards the sacred fire. She must be an unmarried girl under 18 at the time of her appointment, and she agrees to serve until she is 21. The fire she tends is used to burn incense during the rituals.

The Shekinah, or sacred triangle, illuminated by three candles stands in the center of the lodge chamber flanked by seats for the Chaplain and the High Priestess. The members sit in seats along both walls. They wear Masonic-type aprons and other regalia.

Each degree of the Rosicrucian order is prefaced by a solemn oath to keep the secrets of the degree and the activities of the lodge hidden from the uninitiated.

Rosicrucian lodges celebrate two main feasts during the year. The New Year Feast falls on or about March 21 and begins "on the minute when the sign of Aries rises on the horizon on that day in March when the Sun just enters the sign of Aries." The lodge brothers and sisters partake of a symbolic meal of corn, salt, and grape juice. The second feast is the Outdoor Fete around September 23 which is more or less a lodge picnic.

The Rosicrucian Manual (15th edition, 1959) describes the "sacraments" of the cult. For example, there is the Rosicrucian Appellation rite or the naming of an infant. The child must be less than 18 months old and have at least one Rosicrucian parent. Both parents must pledge to have the child educated in non-sectarian schools. "Such ritual may take the place of, or supplant, any christening ceremony" (p. 177).

Children may later (between the ages of 6 and 18 years) join the Junior Order of Torch Bearers. They advance from one unit of the Order to the next as they grow older. The cult furnishes a child-guidance lesson each month for the junior cultists.

The AMORC marriage ceremony must be held within three days after the legal ceremony. It is performed in the Temple by the Master or the Chaplain. Since this service has no legal status, Rosicrucians must undergo a prior civil wedding.

Finally, the cult's burial service is held after noon and preferably in the evening so that it ends about midnight. The deceased is clothed in his lodge apron and the mourners wear not black but purple, the Rosicrucian color of mourning. After the rites the body remains in the Temple until cremation in the morning.

It should be clear by now that any Christian who believes the Rosicrucian statement that the cult does not constitute a religious organization would be disabused of this view if he actually enrolled in the cult or participated in its pagan rites. The *Rosicrucian Manual* claims, "There are high officers in the organization (the AMORC) who are priests, clergymen, rabbis and directors and workers in every one of the various religions throughout the world" (p. 198). We do not know how many misguided Protestant ministers or rabbis have allowed themselves to become enmeshed in this cult, but we would challenge the AMORC to name one Roman Catholic priest in good standing who holds Rosicrucian membership.

(We should point out that the pastor of an Episcopalian church in Dallas, Texas, holds faculty rank in the Rose Croix "University" in San Jose.)

The cult likes to flatter prospective members by pretending that university professors, editors, political leaders, authors, scientists, and other learned men belong to the Rosicrucian order. Its *Mastery of Life* booklet lists Plato, Aristotle, St. Thomas Aquinas, Jesus, Cicero, Dante, Descarte, Benjamin Franklin, and Newton as active Rosicrucians.

The San Jose organization was founded by H. Spencer Lewis, a dabbler in occult lore, who inserted an ad in a New York newspaper in 1915. (The literature of the AMORC refers to this paid ad as a "manifesto.") He had previously directed an outfit known as the New York Institute for Psychical Research. Lewis was born in Frenchtown, New Jersey, in 1883, attended the public schools, and joined the Methodist Church. He claimed to have obtained secret manuscripts of the band of Rosicrucians who established a colony near Philadelphia in 1694. He also went to Europe and claimed to have received authorization from certain French adepts in 1909 to reestablish the order in this hemisphere.

About 100 people replied to the invitation of this first Rosicrucian ad and Lewis was in business. He moved his base of operations from New York to San Francisco to Tampa and finally to San Jose. Lewis died in 1939 and his ashes are interred in the Rosicrucian Park in that city. During his lifetime the chubby, goateed charlatan freely used the title Ph.D. although no one could discover what university had conferred the degree.

One of his four children, Ralph, assumed control of the family business. In the future, control will remain in the male succession of the Lewis family. Ralph Lewis was born in New York City in 1904, attended schools there and a military academy in New Jersey. He skipped college but became Supreme Secretary of the AMORC in 1923.

Ralph Lewis bears the title "Supreme Autocratic Authority" and "Imperator for North, Central and South America, the British Commonwealth and Empire, France, Switzerland, Sweden, and Africa." A five-member Supreme Grand Lodge rubber stamps his decisions.

The younger Lewis is the author of such volumes as *Mental Poisoning* and the *Conscious Interlude*. Most of the books sold by the AMORC continue to be reprints of the works of H. Spencer Lewis. The cult says that these books do not contain the secret teachings of the Rosicrucians, which are reserved for the monthly monographs.

The AMORC has prospered. It now owns a city block in San Jose (population 130,000) and belongs to the local chamber of commerce. Rosicrucian Park includes an administration building, auditorium, Egyptian museum, temple, planetarium, art gallery, library, and science museum. In a recent year the organization reported a payroll in excess of $630,000.

The Lewis cult builds on the legends which inspired the European and early American Rosicrucians, but no link connects the modern AMORC with these earlier occultists. It would be as sensible to maintain that Christopher Columbus founded the Knights of Columbus or that Jehovah established Jehovah's Witnesses.

Nesta H. Webster observes: ". . . nothing is easier than for anyone to make a compound out of Jewish Cabalism and Eastern Theosophy and to label it Rosicrucianism, but no proof whatever exists of any affiliation between the self-styled Rosicrucians of today and the 17th century 'Brothers of the Rosy Cross' " (*Secret Societies and Subversive Movements*, London, 1955).

In his massive 649-page study, *The Brotherhood of the Rosy Cross*, A. E. Waite dismisses the AMORC and similar groups with a single sentence: "They represent individual enterprises which have no roots in the past." In fact, the only mention of the AMORC is given in the preface and it does not even appear in the index. This definitive study was published in 1961 by University Books, New Hyde Park, New York.

Rosicrucianism in its original form got its start from the publication of a pamphlet entitled the *Fama Fraternitatis*. Historians believe its author was Johann Valentine Andrea (1586–1654), a Lutheran theologian. The book was circulated in manuscript form in 1610 and was first printed in Cassel, Germany, in 1614.

The elder Lewis denied that the *Fama Fraternitatis* accomplished anything more than to spark a third or fourth revival of Rosicrucianism in Germany. He insisted that the origin of the cult could be traced to ancient Egypt. Lewis also ridiculed the commonly accepted view that Andrea authored the book. He maintained it was the work of Sir Francis Bacon, "Imperator for the Rosicrucian Order in England." The *Encyclopaedia Britannica* and *Encyclopedia Americana* both attribute the *Fama* to Andrea.

The book describes the adventures of one Christian Rosenkreuz, a fictitious person, who supposedly started the society of Rosicrucians. He was a poor boy who entered a monastery in his early youth and at the age of 16 left on a pilgrimage to the Holy Land in company with one of the monks. The monk, however, fell ill and died on Cyprus and Rosenkreuz continued the journey alone.

He now began a pursuit of mystical and occult knowledge in Damascus, Egypt, and Morocco before returning to Germany. He revealed this secret wisdom to several monks who were sworn to keep it from the profane. Four new members were initiated into the secret society and all the members agreed to heal the sick, appoint a successor to take their place at death, and to keep the existence of the brotherhood secret for 100 years.

Father Christian, as he was called, died at the age of 100 and was buried in an unknown grave. The society of eight members perpetuated itself. Among its traditions was one which said that the grave of the founder would be revealed in 120 years and the brotherhood would be made known to the world. Rosenkreuz' grave was discovered and his body was found to be in a state of perfect preservation.

This was the substance of the romance written by Andrea to advance his own notions of religion and morals. Many simple folk took it seriously, however, and sought admission to the ranks of the secret society. Imposters appeared to claim that they had been initiated into the society of Rosicrucians. From this original legend various groups of alchemists, astrologers, cabalists, Freemasons, and occultists took the general name of "Rosicrucians."

A band of settlers who called themselves Rosicrucians came to American shores and colonized an area near Philadelphia around 1694. By 1801 they had abandoned their buildings and scattered.

Lewis revived interest in Rosicrucianism in the United States, but his group is only the largest of a number of Rosicrucian groups. Another, known as the Rosicrucian Fellowship, was founded by Max Heindel who died in 1919. His widow continued to direct this cult from its headquarters in Oceanside, California, until 1932. The Heindel Rosicrucians mix astrology and traditional Rosicrucianism but do not attempt to operate the large-scale mail-order business of the Lewis cult. Heindel published his occult teachings in various books which are available in larger public libraries.

H. Spencer Lewis did not rest content with tracing his cult back to Rosenkreuz. He maintained that its beginning would be found in the Egypt of Thutmose III in 1500 B.C. Nowadays the cult more modestly states that Rosicrucianism was born during the dynasty of Pharaoh Amenhotep IV about 1350 B.C. Barnum was right.

Catholics would be interested to observe the many similarities between Rosicrucianism, San Jose brand, and the doctrines of Theosophy. Like the AMORC Theosophy teaches that a Great White Brotherhood in remote Tibet directs the dissemination of occult knowledge to a few selected mortals. Both cults teach that our Lord Himself sat at the feet of the adepts of the Great White Brotherhood then headquartered on Mount Carmel. He is said to have traded his human body for the secret wisdom of the GWB. Lewis has written that Jesus — a Gentile not a Jew — and all his Apostles were initiates of the Essenes, whom he identified as a subsidiary of the GWB.

By decree of the Holy Office on July 18, 1919, Roman Catholics were forbidden to join Theosophical societies, take part in their meetings, or read their literature. Theosophist doctrines were declared to be incompatible with Christianity. Presumably the same prohibition would extend to the Rosicrucian cult which propagates a revised Theosophy along with added pagan and superstitious elements.

A careful student of the AMORC, Fr. Hubert Vecchierello, O.F.M., Ph.D., has written:

> But not only is it true that the majority of books published on religious subjects by the Rosicrucians fall under the ban of the Church, because they teach a garbled idea of God, of man, of Jesus Christ, of various beliefs necessary for salvation, etc. It appears to the minds of several weighty canonists who have been approached on this subject, that Rosicrucianism is one of the societies implicitly condemned by the Church, because of its religious teachings, tenets, rituals, prayers, tendencies, etc. (A Catholic Looks at Rosicrucianism, St. Anthony Guild Press, 1939, p. 76).

The elder Lewis recognized the impossibility of anyone trying to remain a Catholic and a Rosicrucian at the same time. "Because of its aggressiveness and its growth, the Order Rosae Crucis of America, as well as in all other countries, has been condemned by the Pope as destructive to the principles of Roman Catholicism" (Rosicrucian Questions and Answers, sixth edition, 1959, p. 245). Lewis went on to explain that his cult had been formally condemned by a papal bull; however, no canon lawyer knows of such a formal condemnation by name and the bull cannot be identified. At any rate this passage indicates that the cult knows full well that the Catholic Church frowns on such occultism and discourages her members from affiliating. No hint that the Church condemns the AMORC will be found in the recruiting literature mailed from San Jose which time and again assures the readers that they will never find anything in Rosicrucianism to disturb their religious orthodoxy.

In answer to another question about the religious affiliation of the principal officers of the AMORC Lewis wrote that most of the officers came from Protestant backgrounds but that "some are members of the Jewish churches (sic) with perhaps an occasional officer who was originally raised or educated in the Roman Catholic Church" (p. 247). The inference is clear: a Catholic would probably not remain a Catholic for long after he became involved in the AMORC.

Canon 1399 warns Catholics against reading books in specifically condemned categories including those favoring superstition or subverting the Christian religion. It would be hard to classify the books and pamphlets of the AMORC as anything else.

Freemasonry perpetuates the Rosicrucian legend by incorporating a Rosicrucian degree in its Scottish rite. In the Southern jurisdiction of the Scottish rite this is the 18th degree of Knight of the Rose Croix of H.R.D.M. Masonic Rosicrucians, of course, have no direct connection with the San Jose organization.

Lewis did reveal that he had asked ten prominent Freemasons to check his cult's constitution before its adoption and publication. Albert Pike, the former Confederate general who remodeled the Scottish rite, became a serious student of oriental religions and occultism, including classic Rosicrucianism.

Similarities between Masonry and the AMORC are many and we suspect that Lewis simply lifted sections of the Masonic ritual for his brainchild. AMORC administers a Great Oath pledging the initiates to secrecy much as does Masonry. The cult provides passwords, secret grips, aprons, and a lodge arrangement not much different from the Masonic lodge.

The basic theological idea of Rosicrucianism is pantheism. In *Rosicrucian Questions and Answers* we read: "The Rosicrucians believe and have always believed that there is but one soul in the universe, and that is the universal soul or the universal consciousness of God" (p. 206). Individuals go through a series of reincarnations but they begin each life cycle with a clean slate. The evil has been purged away but persistent evil tendencies must be curbed by various occult devices.

The early Christian Church was plagued by groups of people known as the Gnostics who claimed to possess secret doctrines from the East. They twisted the words of Christ and formed cells within the Church in which they tried to present their occult interpretations of the Gospel which the mass of ordinary Christians would never understand or appreciate. The Church did its best to uproot these Gnostics and applied the severest penalties of excommunication and condemnation. No thoughtful Christian could pass beyond the first degree of the Rosicrucian cult without realizing that he had been deceived. He was solemnly assured that the AMORC was not a religion and that he would never be urged to accept what was incompatible with his faith. He would soon see that he was becoming involved in a modern Gnosticism totally at odds with the central doctrines of the Christian faith.

The Catholic layman can identify several characteristics of the San Jose cult which would bring it under the ban of his Church. It is a secret society which promotes superstition and offers a slightly modified form of the condemned Theosophy. Its literature obviously falls under the ban of canon law. It imposes oaths just as objectionable to the Christian as those of the Masonic lodges, Mau Mau, tongs, or Mafia. He could not remain a Catholic in good standing and a member of the AMORC.

Even the non-Christian should see that he is wasting $42 a year and valuable time for this mixture of pseudo science, vegetarianism, fantasy, occultism, and humbuggery peddled by the AMORC. Does he really imagine that this California cult possesses secrets of the ages unknown to the scholars and scientists and theologians of the twentieth century? And does he believe that this wisdom can be imparted only to dues-paying subscribers to the AMORC monograph series — and that it ceases to enlighten if it is revealed to those who do not forward $3.50 a month?

CHAPTER 19

MORAL RE-ARMAMENT

*MRA Called "The Salvation Army
of the Upper Class"*

———— • ————

Like a number of other groups discussed in this book, Moral Re-Armament denies it constitutes a separate church or cult. Its adherents may continue to attend other churches as may Rosicrucians, Freemasons, and devotees of the Unity School of Christianity. Nevertheless Moral Re-Armament, or MRA, displays many of the characteristics of a distinct cult and for many it seems to offer a comfortable spiritual home.

MRA does not maintain churches or congregations nor does it ordain ministers. It makes no attempt to provide a ritual of baptism, marriage, or burial for its followers.

MRA seeks to change men. When men change, it believes, the institutions of the world will change. Social disorder will disappear and the problems of labor-management discord, the cold war, and poverty will finally be solved. Communism will lose its appeal and the world will enter an era of peace and prosperity.

To propagate its views MRA uses every media of communication and every public-relations technique. More than 20 million copies of the pamphlet *Ideology and Co-existence* have been distributed to United States and Canadian homes. Another 50 million have been published in various European languages.

A full-length technicolor movie, "The Crowning Experience," played for almost eight weeks in a Times Square theater. The film was based on the life of Mary McLeod Bethune, Negro college president, who joined MRA in her later years.

In 1955 the United States air force provided three planes to transport a 200-member MRA troupe to the Far East, Middle East, and Africa. This troupe put on a play called "The Vanishing Island" which presented the MRA ideology. Later the air force came in for severe criticism for providing official planes for a religious organization.

The pamphlet, the film, and the play all asked for help in the MRA campaign against world Communism. They also frankly seek the allegiance and financial help of all who agree with the MRA approach.

MRA sees itself pitted against Communism as one ideology against another. In fact, MRA spokesmen declare that only MRA can defeat this menace; all other ideologies have failed. MRA emphasizes many basic Christian positions such as the saving powers of Jesus Christ, the sense of sin and evil, the value of prayer, and the guidance of the Holy Spirit. In a sense MRA is a modern example of Protestant pietism and revivalism with some new twists added by founder Dr. Frank Buchman.

Buchman (pronounced Bookman) was born in Pennsburg, Pennsylvania, in 1878 and died in August, 1961. After completing a Lutheran seminary course he was ordained in 1902. He accepted the pastorate of a poor parish and managed to put it on its feet. In the meantime he began to work with young people in an affiliated settlement house, but resigned this position after a disagreement with the trustees over the expenditure of funds.

Buchman went to England and while there was moved by a sermon by a woman evangelist. He determined to put his theoretical Christianity into practice. Back in the States he became a YMCA secretary at what is now Penn State University. Later he became a lecturer at the Hartford Seminary in Connecticut, an interdenominational school.

A dispute with the seminary authorities led Buchman to launch out on his own. He decided to offer his own brand of evangelism to the students of Princeton University. When he accused 85 percent of the Princeton students of sexual perversion — masturbation and homosexuality — he was forbidden the use of campus facilities by the president of the university.

Buchman went to England and applied his counseling and evangelistic techniques on the students at Oxford and Cambridge. At first his group was known as the First Century Christian Fellowship but later it became known as the Oxford Group, although neither Buchman nor his followers had any official connection with that ancient seat of learning. Nor did it bear any relationship to the earlier Oxford Group which under John Henry Newman attempted to Catholicize the Anglican Church. The name "Oxford" Group was used until a meeting in the Black Forest in Germany in 1938 when the new name "Moral Re-Armament" was adopted.

As early as 1918 Buchman had introduced the spiritual house party. The Oxford Group house party was similar to a Catholic weekend retreat. It was often held in the homes of wealthy followers and also in hotels and resorts. The agenda consisted of talks, confessions and testimonials, games and recreation, quiet hours, and common meals. Some were small gatherings of a couple of dozen people but the 1931 house party at Oxford attracted 700 and the 1935 party drew almost 10,000.

Several unfortunate statements by Buchman were interpreted as pro-Nazi and the movement suffered a general decline during the war years. His most famous remark was: "I thank heaven for a man like Adolph Hitler who built a first line of defense against the Anti-Christ of Communism." Buchman did manage to fill the Hollywood Bowl for a MRA rally in 1939 and in 1942 the group acquired its Mackinac Island, Michigan, property.

At Mackinac, one of two training centers, MRA maintains four lodges with accommodations for 1000, a theater, main building, and dining room. The other center is an Alpine retreat at Caux, Switzerland. It was the run-down Palace Hotel which the group acquired and rehabilitated.

Today about 2000 full-time MRA workers serve the movement. They have given all their property to the movement and receive no salary, only room and board and personal expenses. Most converts have been won in England, Germany, and Switzerland and many of the prominent officials are Europeans. Ordinary membership is fluid and informal. "You don't join anything, you don't pay anything, you just begin living the MRA standards." In this respect it is something like the Christophers or Father Lombardi's Better World Movement under Catholic auspices. Certainly the number of MRA sympathizers runs into the hundreds of thousands. The annual budget exceeds two million dollars.

How does MRA propose to change men? Buchman prescribed four techniques: confession, surrender, guidance, and sharing. These four techniques will produce the four absolutes which will transform the world: absolute honesty, absolute purity, absolute selflessness, and absolute love.

The first technique — confession — is the one which has gotten the Buchmanites into the most serious embarrassments. By confession MRA expects a public confession of all personal sins, including sexual offenses. Buchman saw such confession as a therapeutic device which discharged the poison of hidden sins from the soul. The confession of sins in mixed company at the weekend house parties drew criticisms from clergymen as well as psychiatrists.

Following confession to the group or to another person the MRA convert accepts Jesus Christ as his personal savior in the familiar revival manner. He dedicates his efforts to imitate Christ in all things.

In silent meditation the devotee next seeks direct guidance from the Holy Spirit. Walter Houston Clark, who studied the movement, observes: "So far as (MRA) has any central dogma it is that God will give guidance to those who listen for it with the sincere intent to put it into practice." The person living by MRA standards tries to set aside at least 15 minutes a day for a quiet time. During these periods of silence God speaks to him and directs his course of action. He is encouraged to jot down the thoughts which come to him during this period. These quiet times are observed at all MRA house parties and assemblies.

Finally, every Buchmanite agrees to share his faith with others as a missionary. He works alone or as a member of the MRA team. Likewise each MRAer considers himself a soul surgeon and tries to change and reshape the lives of others according to the spirit of Christ.

Beyond these four techniques MRA has no distinctive theology. It comes close to a rather sophisticated fundamentalism with a strong emphasis on conversion. Members are drawn from most of the major Protestant denominations and, despite warnings from the Holy Office and the hierarchy, from the Catholic Church as well.

A number of European political leaders, among them Konrad Adenauer and Robert Schuman, have endorsed the MRA program. Some heads of newly independent African nations support MRA publicly. MRA considers Africa the most important battleground today in the struggle against Communism and directs much of its efforts toward that continent.

Where MRA gets the funds to carry out its extensive propaganda campaign is not altogether clear. Some labor leaders suspect it is subsidized by wealthy industrialists but no proof has been adduced. Certainly MRA makes a stronger appeal to an industrialist than to a laboring man, to a political conservative than to a liberal.

The Catholic Church has taken a dim view of MRA. The Holy Office issued a statement in 1951 which forbade priests and nuns from participating in the movement without express permission from Rome. It also barred Catholic laymen from accepting administrative positions in MRA but did not forbid the laity from joining as members.

Local bishops and hierarchies have taken further steps. Cardinal Hinsley of London prohibited Catholic participation in 1938, and the entire English hierarchy concurred in this ban in 1946. MRA has also been condemned by the hierarchies of Belgium, Ceylon, and the Philippines, and has drawn criticism from various bishops in Germany and Italy.

Recently Cardinal Pizzardo declared: "The Sacred Congregation is astonished to see Catholics and even priests seek certain moral and social objectives, however praiseworthy they may be, in the bosom of a movement which possesses neither the patrimony of doctrine or of the spiritual life, nor the supernatural means of grace which the Catholic Church has."

Bishop Thomas L. Noa, of the Marquette, Michigan, diocese, in which the Mackinac Island training center is located, has issued a pastoral which states that Catholics in his diocese including visitors "may not attend the meetings of MRA or participate in or promote its activities." Bishop Noa has also said: "One cannot help but come to the conclusion that MRA is a modified and borrowed form of Christianity."

MRA does have some Catholic friends besides Adenauer and Schuman. The Swiss bishops have never taken any action against Catholic participation at the Caux headquarters assemblies. The distinguished German theologian, Karl Adam, has written: "Moral Re-Armament is not, as its name might imply, merely an ethical movement, but a religious, indeed in the deepest sense, a Christian movement. But it is in no way a confession or a church community." Dr. George Shuster, former president of Hunter College, wrote favorably about MRA as he observed it in Europe and in his UNESCO position. Strictly speaking, lay Catholics outside the diocese of Marquette or those countries where MRA has been specifically banned may support MRA programs with a clear conscience.

Sir Arnold Lunn has written, "Moral Re-armament is neither a Church nor a Sect. It is a spiritual discipline which all men can practice irrespective of their particular creeds." He reports that a number of conversions to Catholicism, the return of more than 100 lapsed Catholics, and several vocations to the priesthood must be credited to MRA.

Religious indifferentism seems to be the chief danger to the faith which those bishops opposing MRA seek to warn against. MRA apparently ignores the role of the Church and the sacraments and directs its devotees to the inner light. This may also lead to the heresy of illuminism in which every person receives the immediate guidance of the Holy Spirit independent of the authority of the Church.

Whether MRA's simplistic formula to defeat Communism has any real chance of success is also doubtful. Fr. Robert Graham, S.J., writing in *America* magazine, has commented: "The evidence thus far is that MRA has neither the political sophistication nor the doctrinal cohesion that could enable it, at the moment, to cope with Communism as one ideology against another." He added, "Men should be glad if MRA accomplished good for individuals and society; they will be vastly relieved, and even surprised, if it does not do harm to governments or to souls."

Other critics complain that MRA reveals a shallow understanding of the roots of social evils, relies too heavily on slogans and maxims, engages in armchair psychiatry and amateur soul surgery. Its public-relations practitioners have a habit of name dropping and like to stretch innocuous statements by prominent people into enthusiastic endorsements of MRA and its ideology. The movement also makes some extravagant claims of success in various world trouble spots whereas in reality its teams may have played minor or negligible parts as mediators.

For 40 years, from Buchmanism to the Oxford Group to Moral Re-Armament, the movement looked to the direction of Frank Buchman. In the years before his death he had grown increasingly dictatorial and impatient of criticism. His death is a turning point in MRA. No one has taken his place. Whether MRA will survive, much less expand, will probably be decided in the next few years.

CHAPTER 20

I AM

Rapid Decline Marks a Weird Cult
Which Flourished in the 1930's

———— • ————

Despite the embarrassing death (ascension) of founder Guy Ballard and the charges of fraud sustained by a United States court, the once powerful I Am movement continues to attract a few devoted followers. Its heyday has gone.

Ballard's widow, Edna, now 76, maintains homes in Santa Fe, New Mexico, and Chicago where the cult owns a 12-story building in the Loop and a publications center at 8409 Stony Island Avenue. It sponsors regular radio programs on two Chicago stations and staffs reading rooms in a number of large cities. Edna is considered the only Accredited Messenger who can receive messages from the Ascended Masters including Beloved Daddy Ballard. Their son Donald handles the business affairs of the cult.

I first visited the Chicago I Am headquarters about a dozen years ago. In the reading room on the second floor I saw a handful of people studying I Am books and pamphlets. A large painting of George Washington hangs between two garishly colored lithographs of Jesus and St. Germain, the Ascended Master who first revealed I Am doctrines to Ballard in the California mountains. Washington occupies a prominent place in I Am hagiology since Guy disclosed that he had been the father of his country in a previous life; Mrs. Ballard was once known as Joan of Arc.

A motherly looking attendant was discussing the rheumatic ills of a middle-aged devotee when I entered. She finished her conversation and invited me into her office. A huge portrait of Ballard with his gray hair, penetrating eyes, and marble-sized diamond stickpin hung over her desk.

My hostess refused to identify herself — "It doesn't matter who I am." She was reluctant to talk about the organization. "As an outsider you simply would not understand what I would tell you," she said shaking her head in resignation.

"But what do you tell interested inquirers and visitors to your reading rooms about the movement?" I asked.

"All I can say is that I Am teachings represent the final and ultimate religion," she replied. "If the human race does not accept these teachings soon it will have to move to another planet about 4,500,000 miles away." She did not identify the planet.

"No one can make a so-called objective study of I Am," she snapped in response to another question. "Only those who come here through God's direction and with an open will can understand these tremendous truths."

I pointed to several of the unusual pictures decorating the walls and asked her to explain their significance. One showed a woman wearing dozens of red and gold necklaces who sprouted a yellow flame from her forehead and emitted purple rays from her ears. Another showed a bejeweled young man with a similar flame.

My hostess repeated the strange story of Guy Ballard and the Ascended Masters of I Am. From private study and investigation I was able to fill in the details she left out. For example, Ballard was indicted by a Cook County grand jury on March 25, 1929, on a charge of "obtaining money and goods by means of the confidence game." Warrants were never served because he slipped away to the West Coast where he lived for two years under the alias of Dick Gilbert.

Guy Ballard was born in 1878 in Newton, Kansas. He became a spiritualist medium in Chicago but also cultivated an interest in mining. He married Edna Wheeler, a professional harpist and medium, in 1916. A son, Donald, was born in 1918. The couple dabbled in Christian Science, Theosophy, Unity, Rosicrucianism, and other occult groups. Ballard claimed to have spent two years in the Orient between 1919 and 1929 but this is doubted by former associates.

The Ballards had hard sledding. After her husband left for the Coast Mrs. Ballard got a job in a Chicago book shop known as the Philosopher's Nook and operated by her sister. It specialized in occult literature. Mrs. Ballard also edited two periodicals, *American Occultist* and *The Diamond*.

Meanwhile Ballard entered mining engineering in northern California. Through Theosophy he had heard of the existence of the Brotherhood of Masters, or Great Souls, who were supposed to dwell in mountain haunts.

One fine morning, he tells us, he hiked up the side of Mount Shasta and stopped at noon near a mountain spring. He was about to scoop up a cup of cool water when a young man from nowhere appeared and addressed him: "My brother, if you will hand me your cup I will give you a much more refreshing drink than spring water."

Ballard's cup was magically filled with a creamy white liquid. After drinking this potion he experienced an electric-type shock which brought a wonderful sense of well-being. The young man turned out to be the Master St. Germain. He explained that the liquid was Omnipotent Love itself. He revealed to Ballard that in previous lives Ballard had been a famous musician in southern France and a temple priest in ancient Egypt. Then he disappeared.

A few days later, Ballard relates, he received a thin gold card inviting him to revisit the mountain rendezvous. This time his host treated him to some marvelous cakes and he was transported to the realm of the Sahara Desert 70,000 years ago.

On a third occasion a dove delivered another gold invitation to Ballard. This time he left his physical body and flew with St. Germain to the mountainside. St. Germain pushed some boulders aside and they saw majestic rooms filled with precious jewels and gold. A special vault held treasures from the sea which were lost on sunken Spanish galleons. In a sort of mystic movie theater he sat with 70 other Masters and watched the history of the world unfold on a mammoth screen. They witnessed the civilizations of the Gobi and Sahara deserts, the Roman empire, the life of Christ, the story of the lost continents of Mu and Atlantis. The show lasted for hours.

These excursions to the mountain monastery of the Great White Brotherhood continued. Ballard absorbed the principles of the I Am from these monastic mentors. On one holiday they were honored by a visit from seven guests from Venus.

While her husband was enjoying such fascinating experiences in California Mrs. Ballard quietly began to instruct I Am classes in her Chicago home. The Bible of the movement, *Unveiled Mysteries*, was published by the St. Germain Press; Ballard used the pen name Godfre Ray King and shrugged off suggestions that his book was simply a rewrite of a book which had appeared 50 years before entitled *Dweller on Two Planets*.

At this stage the Ballards collaborated closely with William Dudley Pelley, leader of the Fascist Silver Shirts, who was sent to the penitentiary during World War II. The cult has always been intensely nationalistic. Today not one but two American flags fly outside I Am headquarters at 176 W. Washington in Chicago. A framed copy of the Constitution is featured in the book room.

The Ballards staged several rallies in Detroit and Cleveland but hit the big time when they managed to rent and fill the 6000-seat Shrine Auditorium in Los Angeles in 1935. At their public meetings they delivered dictations from St. Germain, Jesus, and other Ascended Masters. In the lobby their agents would sell books, pamphlets, phonograph records, ritual paraphernalia, and pictures. The cult's artist Charles Sindelar announced that Jesus had agreed to sit for 21 days for His portrait which was now available to the public.

Guy Ballard wore only white suits with pink bow ties. Edna swirled onto the stage in a pink evening gown with a diamond wreath, pink cape, and white ostrich feather. Ballard told his audiences that he could make himself invisible at will and that he could dip into lakes of jewels and riches anytime he wanted to. He urged his listeners to call on the purifying Violet Consuming flame but reminded them to remove their hats because otherwise the cosmic light could not penetrate below the chin.

Prof. Charles Braden observes:

> In a scientific age, it [*Unveiled Mysteries*] achieved a remark-
> able circulation and was accepted by literally hundreds of thou-
> sands of American citizens of all classes as true. The movement,
> although it had hard enough times in the beginning, had within
> ten years swept the entire country, captured enormous numbers
> of people in all the great cities, and was claiming more than a
> million followers (*These Also Believe*, p. 262).

The cult developed colorful and spectacular rituals. It established
centers and reading rooms in New York, Philadelphia, Washington,
and, of course, Los Angeles. The Ballards traded their battered
Ford for four cream-colored limousines — black was considered a
taboo color in the world of I Am. By 1938 the Ballards were
traveling with an entourage of 14 people and staying at the best
hotels.

Contributions were called "I Am Love Gifts." Heart-shaped tin
containers bearing the same name were placed near doors and
elevators in I Am centers. The *Los Angeles Times* estimated that the
Ballards averaged $1,000 a day from their class tuition and book sales.

As the movement spread it assumed a more institutionalized
form and observers noticed that the once gracious Mrs. Ballard
assumed a rather haughty and dictatorial attitude. Even devout believers began to refer to her as "Little Dynamite." Heretics were
harshly reprimanded and control of the cult never slipped from the
grip of Guy, Edna, and Donald.

Then in 1939 a new policy was announced. Secrecy was to be the
order of the day. Open sessions were banned. White-uniformed
Minute Men acted as bouncers to eject the uninitiated.

An elite class was developing within the general I Am movement.
These were the Hundred Percenters. To demonstrate their complete
allegiance to the movement they agreed to attend extra study sessions
and to abstain from all meat, onions, garlic, tobacco, liquor, card
playing, and sex activity. Married followers had to separate.

On December 29, 1939, Guy Ballard died of hardening of the
arteries, or, as his wife put it: "Our Blessed Daddy Ballard made his

Ascension last night at 12 o'clock from the Royal Teton Retreat and is now an Ascended Master." His remains were cremated.

But the I Am followers who had often heard Ballard's boasts that he had finally conquered death and disease were not satisfied with this explanation. Many became disillusioned and quit. The new secrecy policy made it difficult to replenish I Am ranks. Ballard's death marked the beginning of the end of the cult as a major American movement.

Six months later another blow fell. A grand jury indicted Edna Ballard and a score of associates on 18 counts. In part, the indictment charged that the defendants "did unlawfully, knowingly, and willfully devise and intend to devise a scheme and artifice to defraud, and for obtaining money and property by means of false and fraudulent representations, pretences and promises from a large number of persons." Ballard was said to have taken in three million dollars during the seven years in which the cult operated under his direction.

A hostile press reported the lengthy and sensational trial and by the time the verdict was given the I Am movement was thoroughly discredited. Mrs. Ballard was found guilty and sentenced to concurrent terms of one year on each of seven counts and fined $8,000. The sentence was suspended. In 1946 the Supreme Court voided the sentence because women had been excluded from the grand jury panel.

Nevertheless the I Am movement is still denied the use of the United States mails and must ship its literature by express. Current I Am publications warn devotees not to try to pay for literature with postal money orders. The notoriety of the trial and the generally critical press have turned the cult into one of the most publicity-shy organizations in the country.

During the trial the I Am leaders castigated the ingratitude of the government since the patriotic I Am-ers by means of powerful mental waves had annihilated three Nazi submarines heading for the Panama Canal, had eliminated 346 enemy spies, and had rendered ineffective the Japanese incendiary balloons sent over the West Coast. Instead of recognition for these contributions the I Am got nothing but abuse and harassment.

To present a logical outline of I Am doctrine is impossible. The Ballards picked up bits and pieces of occultism from scores of sources to fashion their own system. The I Am itself, usually called the Mighty I Am Presence, is called the "individual God Presence" in all people. Some people call the I Am the guardian angel. Each human being possesses an electronic body which abides about 12 to 50 feet above the human body. This electronic body pours light and energy by means of a ray of white light into the top of the head. This light centers in the heart.

To purify the physical body I Am students are asked to call on the Violet Consuming Flame. This flame starts at the feet, flows up through the body to the top of the head, and then to the Mighty I Am Presence. Only the Violet Flame can destroy the residue of evil thoughts and desires which prevent a man from escaping the series of births and rebirths. The Ascended Masters, such as Jesus and St. Germain, used the Violet Flame and were able to escape the limitations of physical life.

Man himself was created perfect and Godlike. He remained so until the close of the first Golden Era which ended about 2,500,000 years ago. From that date on he began to accumulate the impurities, or karma, which chained him to physical reembodiments.

No current membership statistics are available. The 1961 edition of *Purpose of the Ascended Masters "I Am" Activity* booklet, which is an introduction to the cult, speaks of three million to five million followers. This is nonsense. Perhaps 5000 people still give some allegiance to the movement despite the death of Guy Ballard, the trial, the imposed secrecy, and the general disillusionment. As many as 1500 people have been accommodated in the various rooms of the Chicago headquarters.

Late in 1962 I paid another visit to the Chicago I Am center. I could hear a class of I Am students singing a lively hymn in another part of the building. They were probably enrolled in the 14-lesson course in I Am principles advertised on the radio programs.

The receptionist, a lady in her 60's, told me she had been in the movement for more than 25 years. I had not heard much about I Am for some years and inquired if Edna Ballard were still alive.

The lady looked startled and then smiled, "Mrs. Ballard can never die. She could not die if she wanted to." Her answer was given in the same tone of voice she would have used if I had asked if I were in New York or Chicago.

I asked if I could obtain any printed material, but she told me that they had nothing for sale. The truths of I Am could not be bought and sold. Eventually I bought a booklet for 15 cents and a reprint of the February, 1937, issue of the *Voice of I Am* for 75 cents and got 10 cents back from my dollar. All booklets are printed in violet.

As a matter of fact the "offerings" for I Am paraphernalia would discourage the kind of converts who join the Salvation Army. A transparency of "Beloved Saint Germain" with lights sells for $350, and similar lighted pictures are available for Guy, Edna, and Beloved Mary, Mother of Jesus. A series of booklets known as the *I Am Decrees* average $1.25. Some of the titles are *Violet Flame Decrees*, Parts I to IV, *Purity Decrees* (Revised), *Electronic Circle Decrees*, and the *Great Great Silence Decrees*. In I Am terminology, decrees are like prayers except they are demands and commands not petitions.

Large photographs of Guy and Edna dominate the reception room. Edna's photograph must have been taken 25 years ago; her hair style reminds us of matrons in old, old, late, late movies on television. Edna herself visits the Loop center occasionally and conducts the Christmas class for new students.

I Am owns some valuable property, possesses an extensive cultic literature and elaborate ritual, and continues to hold the allegiance of a nucleus of followers. Guy Ballard was such an obvious charlatan that it is hard to believe that hundreds of thousands of people swallowed his stories in the 1930's. Edna will die and the movement will experience another shock. Son Donald will probably not be able to hold the cult together. Perhaps it will disintegrate into local study circles. And perhaps someday some enterprising confidence man will announce to an eager Los Angeles audience that he is the reembodiment of Guy Ballard and has some marvelous things to reveal to those who will pay the price.

CHAPTER 21

NATION OF ISLAM

Mr. Elijah Muhammed
Leads Fanatical Black Muslims

———— • ————

While the rest of the nation mourned the death of 122 passengers, mostly Atlantans, aboard a French airliner in early June of 1962, a leaders of the Black Muslim cult told a rally in Los Angeles that he had not heard such good news for many months.

Minister Malcolm X of the cult's Harlem temple attributed the crash to the will of Allah who was punishing the white devils. A few weeks before a Black Muslim had been killed in a scuffle with police.

Said Malcolm X: "I would like to announce a very beautiful thing has happened . . . (Allah) has answered our prayers over in France. He dropped an airplane out of the sky with over 120 white people on it because the Muslims believe in an eye for an eye and a tooth for a tooth. But thanks to God, or Jehovah, or Allah, we will continue to pray, and we hope that every day another plane falls out of the sky."

Malcolm X, a former convict and dope addict, is probably the best known minister of the fast-growing Negro cult. He heads the New York City temple, one of 50 Muhammad's Temples of Islam in 21 states and the District of Columbia. Estimates of the membership of the Nation of Islam range from 100,000 to over 250,000.

Mr. Elijah Muhammad directs the ersatz Islamic cult from headquarters in Chicago. He recruits followers from the Negroes in the ghettos of large Northern cities. These lower-class Negroes, often recent immigrants from the rural South, find nothing but misery and frustration in their slum surroundings. Unlike the educated upper-

and middle-class Negroes they have no hopes of improving their lot by moving away. They expect to live and die in the Black Belts.

The Nation of Islam offers them an escape. It preaches black supremacy just as the Ku Klux Klan and the White Citizens Councils preach white supremacy. The colored races will soon take control of the world, declares Elijah Muhammad. To do this they must take a firm stand against the white man, the Christian religion, and the Jews. The black man must return to Islam, which is said to be the proper religion for all but the hated whites.

Leading Negro spokesmen such as Ralph Bunche, Roy Wilkins of the NAACP, Thurgood Marshall, and the Rev. Martin Luther King condemn the Black Muslim movement and the hate which animates it. The Black Muslims reject integration and any thought of intermarriage; they seek a total separation of whites and blacks. Muhammad and his followers scorn the NAACP, Urban League, and other Negro middle-class organizations seeking to achieve equal rights.

A mysterious peddler-preacher, who claimed to have come from Arabia, started the movement in Detroit in the early 1930's. Known as Prophet W. D. Fard, he drew on such diverse sources as the Bible, the Koran, the writings of Judge Rutherford of Jehovah's Witnesses, and Freemasonry. He attracted perhaps 8000 Negroes to his banner. Around June, 1934, Fard disappeared and has not been seen since. Today's Black Muslims consider him God or Allah incarnate.

With Fard out of the picture, control of the tiny cult passed to his lieutenant Elijah Muhammad, born Elijah Poole to a Georgia Baptist preacher and his wife. Of limited education he worked at odd jobs and tried his hand at preaching himself. Eventually he affiliated with Fard's cult. Elijah Muhammad moved from Detroit to Chicago in 1934 and established the Allah Temple of Islam.

Muhammad's followers could be numbered in the hundreds for some years. The Communists and the Japanese tried to infiltrate the cult and turn it to their own purposes. Muhammad was jailed from 1942 to 1946 on charges of sedition and inciting his followers to resist the draft. The real growth of the Nation of Islam took place after World War II.

After his release from prison Muhammad returned to Chicago's

South Side and eventually purchased a former synagogue which seats 500. Other temples were operating in Detroit, Milwaukee, and Washington, D. C. He set up the University of Islam, actually a combined grade and high school, which now enrolls 350 children. A similar parochial school educates the children of the cultists in Detroit.

The organization and doctrines of the cult struck a responsive chord in the black ghettos and membership began to balloon. Each member was an active missionary. Black Muslims pass out handbills in front of Christian churches and YMCA's. They hold street-corner meetings, sponsor radio broadcasts, visit pool halls, jails, and barber shops to seek converts.

Finally, publicity in *Time*, *Reader's Digest*, and other national magazines brought the black supremacy movement to public attention. For many years before this it was viewed with concern by Negro leaders, the FBI, and local police departments.

The Black Muslims make a special effort to win converts in prisons. Those who accept Islam must rehabilitate their lives and give up their vices and criminal habits when they get out. C. Eric Lincoln, in his study of the movement, has observed:

> The challenge of an ascetic ideal, balanced by the absence of social barriers to affiliation and service, have brought thousands under the banner of Muhammad. Probably in no other religious organization are alcoholics, ex-convicts, pimps, prostitutes and narcotic addicts welcomed so sincerely (*The Black Muslims in America*, p. 29).

Membership standards are high and many applicants fail to qualify. A stringent moral code forbids drinking and smoking, extramarital sex relations, dope, dancing, sports, gambling, movies. Black Muslims may not eat pork or other specified foods, straighten their hair, use more than a minimum of cosmetics, act in a boisterous or loud manner. They may eat only one meal a day, and chubby Muslims are reprimanded until they diet. Members must give at least 10 percent of their incomes to the Temple.

Black Muslims have been suspended from membership for varying periods of time for dozing during Temple meetings, fraternizing with

Christians, flirting with women, eating corn bread or catfish or other forbidden food.

The sex standards of the Nation of Islam are exceptionally high for people living in their environment. They insist that women Muslims wear modest clothing which covers their legs and arms. Fornication or adultery is cause for immediate dismissal. Women hold no rank in the organization and are outnumbered by men but are tendered great respect.

Black Muslims do not vote in local or national elections but Negro politicians are forced to recognize their power in the Negro community. Muhammad may someday choose to order his followers to vote and no one doubts that he can deliver their votes to friendly candidates. Elijah Muhammad's weekly newspaper column is carried by several Negro papers. He draws crowds of 5000 to 10,000 people on his speaking tours.

Congressman Adam Clayton Powell addressed a rally of the Black Muslims in Harlem in 1963. He urged all Negroes to boycott the NAACP because "whites control it." More than 2,500 listeners cheered him and Malcolm X.

Elijah Muhammad retains full control of the cult although each Temple is under the direction of a Minister. Muhammad has a light complexion himself and could easily pass for an oriental instead of a Negro. He lives in an 18-room mansion in the Hyde Park area of Chicago and owns two Cadillacs and a Lincoln Continental. His whole family is involved in the movement including his wife, six sons, and two daughters. Although he never got past the fifth grade, he is shrewd and clever and knows how to make a strong appeal to the Negroes of the slums.

The Islamic religion propagated by the Black Muslims bears little resemblance to orthodox Islam. Their racial doctrines are at obvious variance with traditional Islam. They ignore such prescriptions as the Ramadan fast. Elijah Muhammad even denies that a white man can embrace Islam even though the Arabs themselves are Caucasians. The Federation of Islamic Associations, the official Moslem organization in this country, has stated that the Black Muslim cult "is not affiliated and is not recognized as truly Moslem."

Some of the cult's doctrines bear a close affinity to those of Jehovah's Witnesses. Man has no soul and is not immortal; only Allah is immortal. There is no heaven or hell. After the coming Armageddon, expected to take place around 1970, the black man will assume his rightful control of this planet.

One of the basic myths of the Black Muslims is that the white man was not created by Allah but was the invention of a black genius called Yakub. When Yakub accomplished this mutation by means of scientific techniques he was cast out of paradise for this crime. This was 6000 years ago. Yakub is also known as Adam, the father of the Caucasians.

In contrast to the white man, a late arrival on the scene, the black man had been on earth since the creation 66 trillion years ago. He is the Original Man.

The wicked white man enslaved the black man, deprived him of his cultural heritage, and imposed an inferior and alien religion, Christianity. Allah appeared in human form in the person of W. D. Fard and appointed Mr. Elijah Muhammad to restore the Negro to his true place and to give him back his ancestral religion, Islam.

The white man even took away the black man's name and substituted a slave name. Each convert to the cult gets a new designation. He keeps his proper name and uses X for his surname. If there are more than one with his name he becomes 2X or 3X.

Black Muslims must attend Temple services two or more times a week. Everyone is thoroughly searched before admittance to a Temple. Any objectionable items such as weapons, cigarettes, liquor are checked at the door. A Muslim usher escorts visitors to their seats. Men sit on the right and women on the left.

At the start of the meeting the Minister gives an Arabic greeting which is returned by the congregation. He may spend a few minutes in Arabic language instruction. Eventually all members should be able to read the Koran in the original language. Unfortunately Muhammad neither speaks nor writes Arabic.

The main feature of the Temple service is the address by the Minister which lasts from two to three hours. He recapitulates Muhammad's teachings. Every half hour the two guards at the front of the auditorium are ceremoniously changed. Only Negroes are admitted to the Temple; white men and Asiatics are politely turned away. Most important meetings are monitored by FBI and police informants.

Within each of the 50 Temples are several "parish" organizations. The Fruits of Islam is a men's paramilitary organization which drills, maintains order at Temple meetings, guards Muhammad, etc. Like all Black Muslims they are forbidden to carry weapons of any kind. Muhammad wants to avoid any riots or bloodshed which would call for a police crackdown. Women Muslims join the Moslem Girls' Training and General Civilization Class.

Highpoint of the year is Saviour's Day on February 26, Fard's birthday anniversary. This holds the same place as Christmas in the Christian churches. Black Muslims exchange cards and attend special services at the Temples.

With the members' tithes the cult conducts its parochial schools, buys and maintains Temples, establishes such businesses as groceries, dry-cleaning establishments, apartment houses, clothing stores, barber shops, gas stations. It hopes to enter manufacturing, perhaps of clothing. The parochial school in Chicago alone costs $40,000 a year to maintain. There are about 1000 adult members of the Chicago Temple. Black Muslims are trying to raise 20 million dollars to build an Islamic Center.

Elijah Muhammad is now 64. One of the jobs of the Fruits of Islam is to protect him from assassination. His successor may be his son Minister Wallace Muhammad of Philadelphia. Malcolm X is a more popular and gifted leader and he may bid for leadership when Mr. Muhammad dies. Such a bid might split the movement.

Another articulate leader is Minister Louis X of Boston. In his late 20's Louis X has written several race plays enacted by the Muslims and presides over a growing congregation. He is a former Episcopalian and his wife a former Catholic.

It is easy enough to laugh at the pretentions of Mr. Elijah Muhammad and the bizarre doctrines he preaches. Nevertheless the Black Muslim movement also stands in judgment on white Christian America. If the Negro in the black ghettos had any ray of hope for a better life for himself and his children, he would turn his back on the crude hate appeals of the Black Muslims. He does not see how the sit-ins, legal decisions, and growth of a Negro upper and middle class affect his own life.

The majority of American Negroes recognize the Black Muslims' solution to the American dilemma as visionary and wholly impractical. Muhammad's demand that the United States government turn over several states to the Negro community to achieve complete separation of the races strikes them as perfectly silly. Nevertheless, we can predict that the Black Muslims will grow several times larger than the present membership before it reaches a plateau.

CHAPTER 22

SECULAR HUMANISM

*Humanist Societies Enroll Only
Minority of American Humanists*

———— • ————

If a pollster could discover the true religious beliefs of a sampling of Americans, he would no doubt find that many who now classify themselves as Protestants and Jews actually fall into a fourth major category of commitment: Secular Humanism. For various reasons millions of people continue to give conventional answers to questions of religious affiliation and to maintain membership in churches for social or ceremonial reasons. Their guiding principles, however, are those of Secular Humanism.

As an organized religious movement Secular Humanism is relatively new. The leading organization, the American Humanist Association, was founded in 1941. But the roots of this religion go back to ancient Greek times, were nourished by such men as Spinoza, and have been invigorated by John Dewey, Bertrand Russell, Sir Julian Huxley, and other modern-day Humanists.

Protagoras in the fifth century B.C. is sometimes considered the first Humanist. He coined the phrase: "Man is the measure of all things, of things that are that they are, and of things that are not that they are not." Renaissance Humanism began in Italy in the fourteenth century and spread to the rest of the continent, but Humanism as we know it remained dormant until the middle of the nineteenth century. The publication of Darwin's *Origin of Species* in 1859 sparked new interest in the this-world philosophy of Humanism.

Humanism today presents itself as a religion, a faith, a commitment, a way of life, but, like Buddhism, it is a nontheistic religion. Humanism is a religion without a God, the supernatural, or sacred scriptures.

Dr. Corliss Lamont, one of Humanism's most persuasive spokesmen, defines religion as a "comprehensive and integrated way of life to which a group of persons give supreme commitment and which includes the shared quest of ideals and celebration of existence. Under this definition naturalistic Humanism, though it rejects belief in any form of the supernatural, is clearly a religion."

Man, not God, is the central concern of the Humanist. A Unitarian minister relates that someone once asked him why he did not believe in a Supreme Being and he replied that he did and that this supreme being was man. For the Humanist this life is the only life men will ever enjoy; immortality is a pleasant myth since man has no soul which might survive the death of his body.

The dedicated Secular Humanist will give assent to a predictable set of beliefs. He will doubtless favor birth control, easier divorce laws, abortion, euthanasia, a ban on capital punishment. He opposes all forms of censorship and probably belongs to the American Civil Liberties Union or other civil liberties groups. He fights what he believes to be encroachment of Church on State, but he is seldom aware that his own position is essentially a religious one and that as such it must stand with Protestantism, Catholicism, and Judaism. On the internationalist scene the Humanist can be expected to support the United Nations, UNESCO, the World Health Organization, disarmament, and ban-the-bomb protests.

To help propagate the religion of Humanism he may elect to join one of the 70 chapters of the American Humanist Association or one of the 28 Ethical Culture Societies in the United States. Many Humanists may also be found in established denominations, especially the Unitarian Universalist, Episcopal, Congregationalist, and Quaker bodies. For a number of reasons seldom related to religious conviction they choose to retain church affiliation even though they are no longer Christians or even theists.

Humanism has managed to capture many of the Unitarian churches in the Midwest and on the West Coast; estimates are that one fifth or one fourth of the Unitarian churches of the country are frankly Humanist. The Unitarians now cooperate with the Universalists in the Council of Liberal Churches. At present these two church bodies enroll about 180,000 people in this country. In 20 years it is not unlikely that the majority of Unitarians and Universalists will be properly classified as Humanists.

A number of Reform and Conservative Jews, including some rabbis, subscribe to basic Humanist positions. They may continue to adhere to Jewish symbols and rites.

The AHA maintains a headquarters at Yellow Springs, Ohio, where it publishes the bimonthly magazine *The Humanist* as well as the *Free Mind* newsletter. Membership dues are only $5 a year and the Association reports about 5000 paid members. Executive director is Edwin H. Wilson, a former Unitarian minister. There are chapters and affiliated groups in 25 states with a majority in California, Illinois, Indiana, Massachusetts, Michigan, New York, and Ohio. A former president of the AHA observes: "Chapters are the beginning of a constructive Humanist 'mass movement' which can eventually offset the educational undertow of fundamentalist supernaturalism and bring to fulfillment the tremendous growth potential of Humanism as an organized movement."

President of the AHA for 1962–1963 was Mrs. Vashti McCollum, of Champaign, Illinois, the plaintiff in the famous McCollum released-time case. Mrs. McCollum objected to the released-time religious education program which embarrassed her son, an agnostic like herself.

Members of AHA chapters find some of the satisfactions in their meetings which orthodox Christians find in church. Depending on state laws the directors of the chapters can be authorized to officiate at marriages and burials. Lamont has written a Humanist funeral service which includes selected classical compositions, poetry readings, meditations, and readings from the New Testament. The service can be adapted for cremation which seems to be the favored form of disposal.

If any name is tied to the founding of organized Humanism in this country, it is that of John Dewey. He is considered something of a patron saint of the AHA. He belonged to the now extinct First

Humanist Society of New York from 1933 until death in 1955. He was also a member of the AHA from its founding. Dewey and a number of other Americans signed the 1933 *Humanist Manifesto* which was a milestone in American Humanism. The *Manifesto* included 15 affirmations:

First: Religious humanists regard the universe as self-existing and not created.

Second: Humanism believes that man is a part of nature and that he has emerged as the result of a continuous process.

Third: Holding an organic view of life, humanists find that the traditional dualism of mind and body must be rejected.

Fourth: Humanism recognizes that man's religious culture and civilization, as clearly depicted by anthropology and history, are the product of a gradual development due to his interaction with his social heritage. The individual born into a particular culture is largely molded by that culture.

Fifth: Humanism asserts that the nature of the universe depicted by modern science makes unacceptable any supernatural or cosmic guarantees of human values. Obviously humanism does not deny the possibility of realities as yet undiscovered, but it does insist that the way to determine the existence and value of any and all realities is by means of intelligent inquiry and by the assessment of their relations to human needs. Religion must formulate its hope and plans in the light of the scientific spirit and method.

Sixth: We are convinced that the time has passed for theism, deism, modernism, and the several varieties of "new thought."

Seventh: Religion consists of those actions, purposes, and experiences which are humanly significant. Nothing human is alien to the religious. It includes labor, art, science, philosophy, love, friendship, recreation — all that is in its degree expressive of intelligently satisfying human living. The distinction between the sacred and the secular can no longer be maintained.

Eighth: Religious Humanism considers the complete realization of human personality to be the end of man's life and seeks its development and fulfillment in the here and now. This is the explanation of the humanist's social passion.

Ninth: In the place of the old attitudes involved in worship and prayer the humanist finds his religious emotions expressed in a heightened sense of personal life and in a co-operative effort to promote social well-being.

Tenth: It follows that there will be no uniquely religious emotions and attitudes of the kind hitherto associated with belief in the supernatural.

Eleventh: Man will learn to face the crises of life in terms of his knowledge of their naturalness and probability. Reasonable and manly attitudes will be fostered by education and supported by custom. We assume that humanism will take the path of social and mental hygiene and discourage sentimental and unreal hopes and wishful thinking.

Twelfth: Believing that religion must work increasingly for joy in living, religious humanists aim to foster the creative in man and to encourage achievements that add to the satisfactions of life.

Thirteenth: Religious humanism maintains that all associations and institutions exist for the fulfillment of human life. The intelligent evaluation, transformation, control, and direction of such associations and institutions with a view to the enhancement of human life is the purpose and program of humanism. Certainly religious institutions, their ritualistic forms, ecclesiastical methods, and communal activities must be reconstituted as rapidly as experience allows, in order to function effectively in the modern world.

Fourteenth: The humanists are firmly convinced that existing acquisitive and profit-motivated society has shown itself to be inadequate and that a radical change in methods, controls, and motives must be instituted. A socialized and co-operative economic order must be established to the end that the equitable distribution of the means of life be possible. The goal of humanism is a free and universal society in which people voluntarily and intelligently cooperate for the common good. Humanists demand a shared life in a shared world.

Fifteenth and Last: We assert that humanism will: (a) affirm life rather than deny it; (b) seek to elicit the possibilities of life, not flee from it; and (c) endeavor to establish the conditions of a satisfactory life for all, not merely for a few. By this positive morale and intention humanism will be guided, and from this perspective and alignment the techniques and efforts of humanism will flow.

Prominent Humanists, although not all members of organized Humanist societies, have included John Galsworthy, Sinclair Lewis, George Santayana, H. G. Wells, James T. Farrell, Thomas Mann, Gilbert Murray, Irwin Edman, Sidney Hook, Erich Fromm, S. I. Hayakawa, George D. Stoddard, Herman J. Muller, Linus Pauling,

Brock Chisholm, Walter Lippmann, Albert Einstein, Sigmund Freud, Archibald MacLeish, Luther Burbank, Prime Minister Nehru, Morris R. Cohen, Max Otto, and Harry A. Overstreet.

Paul Blanshard, author of *American Freedom and Catholic Power* and other books developing the same thesis, is a regular contributor to *The Humanist*. His criticisms of the Catholic Church are based on a Humanist rather than a Protestant philosophy. The AHA Committee on Church and State meets monthly in New York City with Blanshard who is a consultant to the committee. Another literary critic of the Church, the ex-Franciscan priest Emmett McLoughlin, received the "Spirit of Humanism" award from the Cleveland Humanist chapter in 1962.

Humanists are confident that theirs is the religion of the future. They believe that time and science are on their side. The laboratory will one day provide the answers which men have sought and now seek through revelation and sacred books. Service to his fellowmen will replace service to God as the ethical ideal. Man will learn to concentrate on living to the fullest in this life, easing its pain, contributing to its art and beauty.

For the moment Humanists must face the realities of life and its financial demands. Despite the impressive roster of Humanists in science and the arts, the roll call of the AHA is shorter than that of many Catholic parishes. After more than 20 years of organizational work the AHA can claim only about 5000 dues-paying members although millions of Americans share the Humanist viewpoint. And even these 5000 members do not contribute enough to meet the annual $80,000 budget of Humanist House in Yellow Springs. Humanism is supposed to inspire man to devote all his attention to freeing his fellowmen from ignorance, slavery, and disease, but it seems to convert many into free lancers who care little about spreading Humanism or helping the man next door.

The 28 Ethical Culture Societies try "to assert the supreme importance of the ethical factor in all relations of life — personal, social, national and international — apart from any theological or metaphysical considerations." These Societies employ Leaders instead of ministers, but the Leaders perform many of the same functions as clergymen: officiate at weddings and funerals, counsel, name children, etc. The Ethical Culture Societies in New York, Philadelphia, and Chicago operate settlement houses. In New York and Brooklyn the Societies have established high schools with high academic standards which attract a number of non-Ethical Culture students. The national membership of the chapters is 6600. Similar societies have been established in England, Japan, and various countries of Europe.

A variety of old-time free-thought organizations still operate in the United States, but they attract only the village-atheist type. Their publications are crude and anticlerical compared to the magazines and pamphlets of the AHA, but they can be considered a branch of Humanism.

In England the Rationalists are more prominent than the Humanists although the points of view are related. Rationalism has been defined as the "mental attitude which unreservedly accepts the supremacy of reason and aims at establishing a system of philosophy and ethics verifiable by experience and independent of all arbitrary assumptions or authority." In 1957 the British Rationalists changed the name of their monthly magazine to *The Humanist*.

By far the most successful Humanists are the Communists. Some Humanists may seek to disassociate themselves from these Marxists but in their basic premises the Communists are thoroughly Humanist. The Secular Humanists in the United States would no doubt prefer a different political orientation than their Marxist brothers, but with the Communist rejection of God and revelation, concentration on this life, reliance on science and materialism, the great majority of Humanists would have no quarrel. Lamont admits:

> While the Marxist materialists disagree sharply on certain philosophic issues with me and with other Humanists, particularly in their ambiguous attitude toward democratic principles, they are unquestionably humanistic in their major tenets of rejecting the supernatural and the supreme goal, and all religious authority, of setting up the welfare of mankind in this life as the supreme goal, and of relying on science and its techniques (*The Philosophy of Humanism*, p. 21).

Several international Humanist congresses have been held since

World War II. At the first congress in Holland Sir Julian Huxley, biologist and first director general of UNESCO, was elected president of the International Humanist and Ethical Union. A second congress was held in London and a third, in 1962, in Oslo. At this most recent meeting seven national organizations held full membership:

> The American Ethical Union, The American Humanist Association, the Bund Freireligioser Gemeinden (Germany), The Ethical Union (United Kingdom), the Humanistisch Verbond (Belgium), the Humanistisch Verbond (The Netherlands), and the Indian Radical Humanist Movement.

Humanists recognize the need to provide a measure of ritual in their religion *sans* God. Lamont comments: "An essential function for artists and writers in a Humanist society will be to work out rituals and ceremonies that are consistent with the central tenets of Humanism." He points out that it is fairly easy to humanize Christmas, which is commercialized to a great extent anyway. Humanists can celebrate this feast as a "folkday symbolizing the joy of existence, the feeling of human brotherhood and the ideal of democratic sharing." Likewise the Columbia University professor suggests that Humanists can observe Easter as a "rebirth of the vital forces of Nature and the renewal of man's own energies."

The potential for organized Secular Humanism is enormous, but whether the existing Humanist groups will be able to tap this potential is doubtful. The appeal so far has been to the intelligentsia, the scientist, and the scholar. Many Americans of average IQ and ability no longer accept the formularies of Christianity and Judaism but will either continue to hold church membership for a variety of reasons or will live by their own personal brand of materialism. The potential Humanist now driving a bus, pumping gas, typing letters, or tending an assembly line will find himself in deep intellectual waters if he dips into the pages of *The Humanist* or drops into a Humanist lecture. The only mass movement inculcating Humanism with a degree of success is Communism; Humanists in the free world would rather not be reminded of this philosophical kinship.

SELECTED BIBLIOGRAPHY

General

Algermissen, Konrad, *Christian Sects* (New York: Hawthorn, 1962).

Atkins, Gaius Glenn, *Modern Religious Cults and Movements* (New York: Fleming H. Revell, 1923).

Bach, Marcus, *They Have Found a Faith* (Indianapolis: Bobbs-Merrill, 1946).

Braden, Charles S., *These Also Believe* (New York, Macmillan, 1949).

Clark, E. T., *The Small Sects in America* (New York and Nashville: Abingdon-Cokesbury, 1949).

Davies, Horton, *The Challenge of the Sects* (Philadelphia: Westminster, 1961).

Ferguson, Charles W., *The Confusion of Tongues* (New York: Doubleday, Doran, 1928).

Hardon, John A., *The Protestant Churches of America* (Westminster, Md.: Newman, 1958).

Martin, Walter R., *The Rise of the Cults* (Grand Rapids: Zondervan, 1955).

Mathison, Richard, *Faiths, Cults and Sects of America, From Atheism to Zen* (Indianapolis: Bobbs-Merrill, 1960).

Mayer, F. E., *Religious Bodies of America* (St. Louis: Concordia, 1961).

Mead, Frank S., *Handbook of Denominations in the United States*, 2 rev. ed. (New York and Nashville: Abingdon-Cokesbury, 1961).

Van Baalen, J. K., *The Chaos of Cults* (Grand Rapids: Eerdmans, 1960).

Weigel, Gustave, *Churches in North America* (Baltimore: Helicon, 1961).

Whalen, William J., *Separated Brethren*, rev. ed. (Milwaukee: Bruce, 1961).

Doukhoborism

Hawthorn, Harry B., ed., *The Doukhobors of British Columbia* (Vancouver: University of British Columbia and J. M. Dent [Canada], 1955).

Wright, J. F. C., *Slava Bohu: The Story of the Doukhobors* (New York: Farrar & Rinehart, 1940).

Swedenborgianism

Swedenborg, Emanuel, *The True Christian Religion* (London and New York: J. M. Dent and E. P. Dutton, 1933).

Toksvig, Signe, *Emanuel Swedenborg* (New Haven, Conn.: Yale University Press, 1948).
Trowbridge, George, *Swedenborg: Life and Teaching* (New York: Swedenborg Foundation, 1944).

Freemasonry

Box, Hubert S., *The Nature of Freemasonry* (London: Augustine Press, 1952).
Graebner, Theodore, *Is Masonry a Religion?* (St. Louis: Concordia, 1946).
Hannah, Walton, *Darkness Visible* (London: Augustine Press, 1952).
——— *Christian by Degrees* (London: Augustine Press, 1954).
Mackey, Albert G., *Encyclopedia of Freemasonry* (Philadelphia: L. H. Everts, 1887).
Pick, Fred L., and Knight, G. Norman, *The Pocket History of Freemasonry* (New York: Philosophical Library, 1953).
Preuss, Arthur, *A Study in American Freemasonry* (St. Louis: Herder, 1908).
Whalen, William J., *Christianity and American Freemasonry* (Milwaukee: Bruce, 1958).

Mormonism

Arbaugh, George B., *Revelation in Mormonism* (Chicago: University of Chicago Press, 1932).
Brodie, Fawn M., *No Man Knows My History* (New York: Knopf, 1946).
Hinckley, Gordon B., *What of the Mormons?* (Salt Lake City: Church of Jesus Christ of Latter-day Saints, 1954).
Linn, W. A., *The Story of the Mormons* (London and New York: Macmillan, 1902).
O'Dea, Thomas F., *The Mormons* (Chicago: University of Chicago Press, 1957).
Smith, Joseph, *The Book of Mormon: Doctrine and Covenants; The Pearl of Great Price* (Salt Lake City: Church of Jesus Christ of Latter-day Saints).
Talmadge, James E., *Articles of Faith* (Salt Lake City: Church of Jesus Christ of Latter-day Saints, 1952).
West, Ray B., *Kingdom of the Saints* (New York: Viking, 1957).

Baha'i

The Baha'i Community: A Summary of Its Foundation and Organization (Wilmette, Ill.: National Spiritual Assembly, 1947).
Esslemont, J. E., *Baha'u'llah and the New Era* (Wilmette, Ill.: Baha'i Publishing Committee, 1952).

White, Ruth, *Baha'i Leads out of the Labyrinth* (New York: Universal, 1944).

Spiritualism

Lawton, George S., *The Drama of Life After Death* (New York: Henry Holt, 1932).
Spiritualist Manual (Washington, D. C.: National Spiritualist Association, 1944).
Thurston, Herbert, *The Church and Spiritualism* (Milwaukee: Bruce, 1932).

Seventh-day Adventism

Herndon, Booton, *The 7th Day: The Story of the Seventh-day Adventists* (New York: McGraw-Hill, 1960).
Martin, Walter R., *The Truth About Seventh Day Adventism* (Grand Rapids: Zondervan, 1960).
Nichol, Francis D., *The Midnight Cry* (Washington, D. C.: Watford, Stanborough Press, 1944).
———— *Reasons for Our Faith* (Washington, D. C.: Review and Herald Publishing Co., 1947).
Questions on Doctrine (Takoma Park: Review and Herald Publishing Co., 1957).

New Thought

Dresser, Horatio W., *A History of the New Thought Movement* (New York: Thomas Y. Crowell, 1919).
Holmes, Ernest, *New Thought Terms and Their Meanings* (New York: Dodd, Mead, 1942).

Christian Science

Bates, Ernest Sutherland, and Dittemore, John V., *Mary Baker Eddy, the Truth and the Tradition* (London: George Routledge and Sons, 1933).
Beasley, Norman, *The Cross and the Crown: The History of Christian Science* (New York: Duell, Sloan and Pearce, 1952).
Bellwald, A. M., *Christian Science and the Catholic Faith* (New York: Macmillan, 1922).
Braden, Charles S., *Christian Science Today* (Dallas: Southern Methodist University Press, 1958).
Dakin, Edwin F., *Mrs. Eddy: the Biography of a Virginal Mind* (New York: Scribner's, 1929).
Eddy, Mary Baker, *Science and Health with Key to the Scriptures* (Boston: Christian Science Publishing Society).

Peel, Robert, *Christian Science: Its Encounter with American Culture* (New York: Holt, 1958).

Powell, Lyman P., *Mary Baker Eddy* (New York: Lyman P. Powell, 1930).

Wilbur, Sybil, *The Life of Mary Baker Eddy* (Boston: Christian Science Publishing Society, 1938).

Old Catholicism

Bartoszek, Donald S., *Episcopi Vagantes, Old Catholics and Their Recent Counterparts in the United States of America*, unpublished master's thesis (Chicago: Mundelein Seminary, 1960).

Moss, C. B., *The Old Catholic Movement* (London: S.P.C.K., 1948).

Jehovah's Witnesses

Cole, Marley, *Jehovah's Witnesses: The New World Society* (New York: Vantage, 1955).

Hebert, Gerard, *The Witnesses of Jehovah* (Paterson, N. J.: St. Anthony Guild Press, 1963).

Jehovah's Witnesses in the Divine Purpose (Brooklyn: Watchtower Bible and Tract Society, 1959).

"Let God Be True" (Brooklyn: Watchtower Bible and Tract Society, 1952).

Pike, Royston, *Jehovah's Witnesses* (New York: Philosophical Library, 1954).

Stroup, Herbert H., *Jehovah's Witnesses* (New York: Columbia University Press, 1945).

Whalen, William J., *Armageddon Around the Corner: A Report on Jehovah's Witnesses* (New York: John Day, 1962).

Salvation Army

Neal, Harry Edward, *The Hallelujah Army* (Philadelphia: Chilton, 1961).

Nygaard, Norman E., *Trumpet of Salvation: The Story of William and Catherine Booth* (Grand Rapids: Zondervan, 1961).

Unity School of Christianity

Bach, Marcus, *The Unity of Life* (Englewood Cliffs, N. J.: Prentice Hall, 1962).

Cady, H. Emilie, *Lessons in Truth* (Lee's Summitt, Mo.: Unity School of Christianity, 1954).

Freeman, James Dillet, *The Story of Unity* (Lee's Summit, Mo.: Unity School of Christianity, 1954).

Pentecostalism

Gee, Donald, *The Pentecostal Movement* (London: Elim Publishing Co., 1949).

Redford, M. E., *The Rise of the Church of the Nazarene* (Kansas City, Mo.: Nazarene Publishing House, 1951).

Winehouse, Irwin, *The Assemblies of God, a Popular Survey* (New York: Vantage, 1959).

Polish National Catholicism

Andrews, Theodore, *The Polish National Catholic Church in America and Poland* (London: S.P.C.K., 1953).

Fox, Paul, *The Polish National Catholic Church* (Scranton: School of Christian Living, n.d.).

Theosophy and the Liberal Catholic Church

Blavatsky, Helena P., *Isis Unveiled* and *The Secret Doctrine*, various editions.

———— *The Key to Theosophy* (Adyar, Madras, India: Theosophical Publishing Society, 1956).

Martindale, C. C., *Theosophy* (London: Catholic Truth Society, 1956).

Ransome, Josephine, *A Short History of the Theosophic Society* (Adyar, Madras, India: Theosophical Publishing Society, 1938).

Symonds, John, *The Lady With the Magic Eyes: Madame Blavatsky — Medium and Magician* (New York: Thomas Yoseloff, 1960).

Williams, Gertrude Marvin, *Priestess of the Occult* (New York, 1946).

Aglipayanism

Achutegui, Pedro S. de, and Bernad, Miguel Anselmo, *Religious Revolution in the Philippines* (Manila: Ateneo de Manila, 1960).

Whittemore, Lewis Bliss, *Struggle for Freedom* (Greenwich, Conn.: Seabury Press, 1961).

Rosicrucianism

Lewis, H. Spencer, *Rosicrucian Manual* (San Jose, Calif.: Supreme Grand Lodge of AMORC, 1959).

———— *Rosicrucian Questions and Answers, with Complete History* (San Jose, Calif.: Supreme Grand Lodge of AMORC, 1959).

Moral Re-Armament

Clark, Walter Houston, *The Oxford Group: Its History and Significance* (New York: Bookman Associates, 1951).

Eister, Allan W., *Drawing Room Conversion: A Sociological Account* of the Oxford Group Movement (Durham, N. C.: University of North Carolina Press, 1950).

Howard, Peter, Frank Buchman's Secret (Garden City, N. Y.: Doubleday, 1961).

Lunn, Arnold, Enigma: A Study of Moral Rearmament (London: Longmans, 1957).

I Am

King, Godfre Ray (Guy Ballard) Unveiled Mysteries (Chicago: St. Germain Press, 1934).

Bryan, Gerald B., Psychic Dictatorship in America (Los Angeles: Truth Research Publications, 1940).

Nation of Islam

Essien-Udom, E. U., Black Nationalism (Chicago: University of Chicago Press, 1962).

Lincoln, C. Eric, The Black Muslims in America (Boston: Beacon, 1961).

Secular Humanism

Lamont, Corliss, The Philosophy of Humanism, 4 rev. ed. (New York: Wisdom Library, 1957).

Morain, Lloyd and Mary, Humanism as the Next Step (Boston: Beacon, 1954).

INDEX